Holidays in Eastern France

Matilda Betham-Edwards

Contents

PREFACE. 7

CHAPTER I. THE VALLEY OF THE MARNE.. 9

CHAPTER II. NOISIEL: THE CITY OF CHOCOLATE. 25

CHAPTER III. PROVINS AND TROYES. 43

CHAPTER IV. AMONG FRENCH PROTESTANTS AT MONTBELIARD 52

CHAPTER V. ST. HIPPOLYTE, MORTEAU, AND THE SWISS BORDERLAND. 64

CHAPTER VI. BESANCON AND ITS ENVIRONS.. 72

CHAPTER VII ORNANS, COURBET'S COUNTRY, AND THE VALLEY ....
   OF THE LOUE. 87

CHAPTER VIII. SALINS, ARBOIS, AND THE WINE COUNTRY OF THE JURA. 92

CHAPTER IX. LONS-LE-SAUNIER.. 101

CHAPTER X. CHAMPAGNOLE AND MOREZ. 111

CHAPTER XI. ST. CLAUDE: THE BISHOPRIC IN THE MOUNTAINS...................... 119

CHAPTER XII. NANTUA AND THE CHURCH OF BRON........................... 128

APPENDIX. 136

HOLIDAYS IN EASTERN FRANCE

BY

Matilda Betham-Edwards

PREFACE.

Travelling in France without hotels, or guide-books, might, with very little exaggeration, be chosen as a title to this volume, which is, indeed, the record of one visit after another among charming French people, and in delightful places, out of the ordinary track of the tourist. Alike in the valley of the Marne--amongst French Protestants at Montbeliard--at Besancon amid the beautiful scenery of the Doubs--at Lons-le-Saunier, from whence so many interesting excursions were made into the Jura--in the very heart of the Jura highlands--at Champagnole, Morez, and St. Claude, it was my good fortune to see everything under unique and most favourable auspices, to be no tourist indeed, but a guest, welcomed at every stage, and pioneered from place to place by educated ladies and gentlemen delighted to do the honours of their native place. Thus it came about that I saw, not only places, but people, and not only one class, but all, peasant and proprietor, Protestant and Catholic, the bourgeoisie of the towns, the mountaineers of the highlands, the schoolmaster, the pastor, the cure. Wherever I went, moreover, I felt that I was breaking new ground, the most interesting country I visited being wholly unfamiliar to the general run of tourists, for instance, the charming pastoral scenery of Seine and Marne, the picturesque valleys of the Doubs and the Loue, and the environs of Montbeliard and Besancon, the grand mountain fastnesses, close-shut valleys, or combes, the solitary lakes, cascades, and torrent rivers of the Jura.

Many of the most striking spots described in these pages are not even mentioned in Murray, whilst the difficulty of communication renders them comparatively unknown to the French themselves, only a few artists having as yet found them out. Ornans--Courbet's birth and favourite abiding place, in the valley of the Loue--is one of these. St. Hippolyte, near Montbeliard, is another, and a dozen more might be named equally beautiful, and, as yet, equally unknown. New lines of railway, however, are to be opened within the next few years in several directions, and thus the delightful scenery of Franche-Comte will, ere long, be rendered accessible to all. For the benefit of those travellers who are undaunted by difficulties, and prefer to go off the beaten track even at the risk of encountering discomforts, I have reprinted, with many additions, the following notes of visits and travel in the most interesting part of Eastern France, which, in part, originally appeared in "Frazer's Magazine," 1878.

In a former work, "Western France," I treated of a part of France which was ultra-Catholic; in this one I was chiefly among the more Protestant districts of the whole country, and it may be interesting to many to compare the two.

CHAPTER I.
THE VALLEY OF THE MARNE.

How delicious to escape from the fever heat and turmoil of Paris during the Exhibition to the green banks and sheltered ways of the gently undulating Marne! With what delight we wake up in the morning to the noise, if noise it can be called, of the mower's scythe, the rustle of acacia leaves, and the notes of the stock-dove, looking back as upon a nightmare to the horn of the tramway conductor, and the perpetual grind of the stone-mason's saw. Yes! to quit Paris at a time of tropic heat, and nestle down in some country resort is, indeed, like exchanging Dante's lower circle for Paradise. The heat has followed us here, but with a screen of luxuriant foliage ever between us and the burning blue sky, and with a breeze rippling the leaves always, no one need complain.

With the cocks and the hens, and the birds and the bees, we are all up and stirring betimes; there are dozens of cool nooks and corners if we like to spend the morning out of doors, and do not feel enterprising enough to set out on an exploring expedition by diligence or rail. After the midday meal everyone takes a siesta, as a matter of course, waking up between four and five o'clock for a ramble; wherever we go we find lovely prospects. Quiet little rivers and canals winding in between lofty lines of poplars, undulating pastures and amber cornfields, picturesque villages crowned by a church spire here and there, wide sweeps of highly cultivated land interspersed with rich woods, vineyards, orchards and gardens--all these make up the scenery familiarized to us by some of the most characteristic of French painters.

Just such tranquil rural pictures have been portrayed over and over again by Millet, Corot, Daubigny, and in this very simplicity often lies their charm. No costume or grandiose outline is here as in Brittany, no picturesque poverty, no poetic archaisms; all is rustic and pastoral, but with the rusticity and pastoralness of every day.

We are in the midst of one of the wealthiest and best cultivated regions of France moreover, and, when we penetrate below the surface, we find that in manner and customs, as well as dress and outward appearance, the peasant and agricultural population, generally, differ no little from their remote country-people, the Bretons. In this famous cheese-making country, the "Fromage de Brie" being the speciality of these rich dairy farms, there is no superstition, hardly a trace of poverty, and little that can be called poetic. The people are wealthy, laborious, and progressive. The farmers' wives, however hard they may work at home, wear the smartest of Parisian bonnets and gowns when paying visits. I was going to say when at church, but nobody does go here!

It is a significant fact that in the fairly well to do educated district, where newspapers are read by the poorest, where well-being is the rule, poverty the exception, the church is empty on Sunday, and the priest's authority is nil. The priests may preach against abstinence from church in the pulpits, and may lecture their congregation in private, no effect is thereby produced. Church-going has become out of date among the manufacturers of Brie cheese. They amuse themselves on Sundays by taking walks with their children, the pater-familias bathes in the river, the ladies put on their gala dresses and pay visits, but they omit their devotions.

Some of these tenant-farmers, many of the farms being hired on lease, possessors of small farms hiring more land, are very rich, and one of our neighbours whose wealth had been made by the manufacture of Brie cheese lately gave his daughter a 100,000 francs, L40,000, as a dowry. The wedding breakfast took place at the Grand Hotel, Paris, and a hundred guests were invited to partake of a sumptuous collation. But in spite of fine clothes and large dowries, farmers' wives and daughters still attend to the dairies, and, when they cease to do so, doubtless farming in Seine et Marne will no longer be the prosperous business we find it. It is delightful to witness the wide-spread well-being of this highly-farmed region.

"There is no poverty here," my host tells me, "and this is why life is so pleasant."

True enough, wherever you go, you find well-dressed, contented-looking people, no rags, no squalor, no pinched want. Poverty is an accident of rare occurrence, and not a normal condition, everyone being able to get plenty of work and good pay. The habitual look of content written upon every face is very striking. It seems as if in this land of Goshen, life were no burden, but matter of satisfaction only, if not of thankfulness. Class distinction can hardly be said to exist; there are employers and employed, masters and servants, of course, but the line of demarcation is lightly drawn, and we find an easy familiarity wholly free from impoliteness, much less vulgarity, existing between them.

That automatic demureness characterizing English servants in the presence of their employers, is wholly unknown here. There are households with us where the servants might all be mutes for any signs of animation they give, but here they take part in what is going on, and exchange a word and a smile with every member of the household, never dreaming that it should be otherwise. One is struck too here by the good looks, intelligence, and trim appearance of the children, who, it is plain, are well cared for. The houses have vines and sweet peas on the wall, flowers in the window, and altogether a look of comfort and ease found nowhere in Western France. The Breton villages are composed of mere hovels, where pigs, cows, and poultry live in close proximity to their owners, a dung-hill stands before every front door, and, to get indoors and out, you have always to cross a pool of liquid manure. Here order and cleanliness prevail, with a diffusion of well-being, hardly, I should say, to be matched out of America.

Travellers who visit France again and again, as much out of sympathy with its people's institutions as from a desire to see its monuments and outward features, will find ample to reward them in Seine et Marne. On every side we have evidence of the tremendous natural resources and indefatigable laboriousness of the people. There is one point here, as elsewhere in France, which strikes an agriculturist with astonishment, and that is the abundance of trees standing amid cornfields and miscellaneous crops, also the interminable plantation of poplars that can be seen on every side, apparently without any object. But the truth is, the planting of apple and pear trees in fields is no extravagance, rather an economy, the fruit they produce exceeding in value the corn they damage, whilst the puzzling line of poplars growing beside canals and rivers is the work of the Government, every spare bit of ground belonging to the State being planted with them for the sake of the timber. The crops are splendid partly owing to the soil, and partly to the advanced system of agriculture. You may see exposed for sale, in little towns, the newest American agricultural implements, whilst the great diversity of products speaks volumes for the enterprise of the farmers.

As you stroll along, now climbing, now descending this pleasantly undulated country, you may see growing in less than an acre, a patch of potatoes here, a vineyard there, on one side a bit of wheat, oats, rye, and barley, with fruit-trees casting abundant shadow over all; on the other Indian corn, clover and mangel-wurzel in the green state, recently planted for autumn fodder; further on a poppy field, three weeks ago in full flower, now having full pods ready for gathering--the opium poppy being cultivated for commerce here--all these and many more are found close together, and near them many a lovely little glen, copse, and ravine, recalling Scotland and Wales, while the open hill-sides show broad belts of pasture, corn and vineyard. You may walk for miles through what seems one vast orchard, only, instead of turf, rich crops are growing under the trees. This is indeed the orchard of France, on which we English folk largely depend for our summer fruits. A few days ago the black-currant trees were being stripped for the benefit of Parisian lovers of cassis, a liqueur in high repute.

We encounter on our walks carts laden with plums packed in baskets and barrels on their way to Covent Garden. Later on, it will be the peach and apricot crops that are gathered for exportation. Later still, apples, walnuts, and pears; the village not far from our own sends fruit to the Paris markets valued at 1,000,000 francs annually, and the entire valley of the Marne is unequalled throughout France for fruitfulness and abundance. But the traveller must settle down in some delicious retreat in the valley of the Marne to realize the interest and charm of such a country as this. And he must above all things be a fairly good pedestrian, for, though a land of Goshen flowing with milk and honey, it is not a land of luxuries, and carriages, good, bad, or indifferent, are difficult to be got. A countless succession of delightful prospects is offered to the persevering explorer, who, each day, strikes out in an entirely different direction. I have always been of opinion that the best way to see a country is to make a halt in some good central point for weeks at a time, and from thence "excursionize." By these means, much fatigue is avoided, and the two chief drawbacks to the pleasure of travel, namely, hotels and perpetual railway travel, are avoided as much as possible.

Seine et Marne, if not one of the most picturesque regions in France, abounds in those quiet charms that grow upon the sympathetic traveller. It is not a land of marvels and pictorial attractions like Brittany. There is no costume, no legendary romance, no stone array of Carnac to entice the stranger, but, on the other hand, the lover of nature, in her more subdued aspects, and the archaeologist also, will find ample to repay them. It is not my intention to give a history of the ancient cities and towns visited during my stay, or, indeed, to offer an itinerary, or any other kind of information so amply provided for us in English and foreign Handbooks. My object is merely to relate my own experiences in this and other Eastern regions of France, for, if these are not worth having, no rechauffe of facts, gleaned here and there, can be so; and I also intend only to quote other authors when they are inaccessible to the general reader.

With regard, therefore, to the history of the departement of Seine et Marne, constructed, in 1790, from the province of Brie, also from the Ile de France, and the so called Gatinois Francais, I will say a few words. Although it only boasts of two important historical monuments, namely, the Cathedral of Meaux and the Chateau of Fontainebleau; scattered about the country are noteworthy remains of different epochs, Celtic, Roman, Merovingian, mediaeval; none, perhaps, of paramount importance, but all interesting to the archaeologist and the artist. Such remains as those of the Merovingian crypt at Jouarre, and the various monuments of Provins, well repay the traveller who visits these places on purpose, whilst, as he zig-zags here and there, he will find many a village church of quaint exterior and rich Gothic decoration within. Fontainebleau, being generally included in a visit to Paris, I do not attempt to describe, but prefer to lead the traveller a little off the ordinary track, on which, indeed, he wants no guide but Murray and Joanne.

My rallying point was a pleasant country-house at Couilly, offering easy opportunity of studying agriculture and rural life, as well as of making excursions by road and rail. Couilly itself is charming. The canal, winding its way between thick lines of poplar trees towards Meaux, you may follow in the hottest day of summer without fatigue. The river, narrow and sleepy, yet so picturesquely curling amid green slopes and tangled woods, is another delightful stroll; then there are broad, richly wooded hills rising above these, and shady side-paths leading from hill to valley, with alternating vineyards, orchards, pastures, and cornfields on either side. Couilly lies in the heart of the cheese-making country, part of the ancient province of Brie from which this famous cheese is named.

The Comte of Brie became part of the French kingdom on the occasion of the marriage of Jeanne of Navarre with Philip-le-Bel in 1361, and is as prosperous as it is picturesque. It also possesses historic interest. Within a stone's throw of our garden wall once stood a famous convent of Bernardines, called Pont-aux-Dames. Here Madame du Barry, the favourite of Louis XV., was exiled after his death; on the outbreak of the Revolution, she flew to England, having first concealed, somewhere in the Abbey grounds, a valuable case of diamonds. The Revolution went on its way, and Madame du Barry might have ended her unworthy career in peace had not a sudden fit of cupidity induced her to return to Couilly when the Terror was at its acme, in quest of her diamonds. The Committee of Public Safety got hold of Madame du Barry, and she mounted the guillotine in company of her betters, showing a pusillanimity that befitted such a career. What became of the diamonds, history does not say. The Abbey of Pont-aux-Dames has long since been turned to other purposes, but the beautiful old-fashioned garden still remains as it was.

Couilly, like most of the ancient villages in Seine et Marne, possesses a church of an early period, though unequal in interest to those of its neighbours. It is also full of reminiscences of the last Franco-German war. My friend's house was occupied by the German commander and his staff, who, however, committed no depredations beyond carrying off the bed-quilts and blankets, a pardonable offence considering the excessive cold of that terrible winter.

Not far off, on a high hill, is a farm-house, known as the Maison Blanche, in which Jules Favre gave utterance to the memorable words: "Not an inch of our territory--not a stone of our fortresses," when in conference with Bismarck and Moltke in 1870. It is said that a peasant who showed them the way meditated assassinating all three, and was only prevented by the fear of his village being made the scene of vengeance. Already, German tourists are finding their way back to these country resorts, and the sound of the German tongue is no longer unbearable to French ears. It is to be hoped that this outward reconciliation of the two nationalities may mean something deeper, and that the good feeling may increase.

The diligence passes our garden gate early in the morning, and in an hour and a half takes us to Meaux, former capital of the province of La Brie, bishopric of the famous Bossuet, and one of the early strongholds of the Reformation. The neighbouring country, pays Meldois as it is called, is one vast fruit and vegetable garden, bringing in enormous returns. From our vantage ground, for, of course, we get outside the vehicle, we survey the shifting landscape, wood and valley and plain, soon seeing the city with its imposing Cathedral, flashing like marble, high above the winding river and fields of green and gold on either side. I know nothing that gives the mind an idea of fertility and wealth more than this scene, and it is no wonder that the Prussians, in 1871, here levied a heavy toll; their sojourn at Meaux having cost the inhabitants not less than a million and a half of francs. All now is peace and prosperity, and here, as in the neighbouring towns, rags, want, and beggary are not found. The evident well-being of all classes is delightful to behold.

Meaux, with its shady boulevards and pleasant public gardens, must be an agreeable place to live in, nor would intellectual resources be wanting. We strolled into the spacious town library, open, of course, to all strangers, and could wish for no better occupation than to con the curious old books and the manuscripts that it contains. One incident amused me greatly. The employe, having shown me the busts adorning the walls of the principal rooms, took me into a side closet, where, ignominiously put out of sight, were the busts of Charles the Tenth and Louis-Philippe.

"But," said our informant, "we have more busts in the garret. The Emperor Napoleon III., the Empress and the Prince Imperial!"

Naturally enough, on the proclamation of the Republic, these busts were considered at least supererogatory, and it is to be hoped they will stay where they are. The Eveche, or Bishop's Palace, is the principal sight at Meaux. It is full of historic associations, besides being very curious in itself. Here have slept many noteworthy personages, Louis XVI. and Marie Antoinette when on their return from Varennes, June 24th, 1791, Napoleon in 1814, Charles X. in 1828, later, General Moltke in 1870, who said upon that occasion,

"In three days, or a week at most, we shall be in Paris;" not counting on the possibilities of a siege.

The room occupied by the unfortunate Louis XVI and his little son, still bears the name of "La Chambre du Roi," and cannot be entered without sadness. The gardens, designed by Le Notre, are magnificent and very quaint, as quaint and characteristic, perhaps, as any of the same period; a broad, open, sunny flower-garden below, above terraced walks so shaded with closely-planted plane trees that the sun can hardly penetrate them on this July day. These green walks, where the nightingale and the oriole were singing, were otherwise as quiet as the Eveche itself; but the acme of quiet and solitude was only to be found in the avenue of yews, called Bossuet's Walk. Here it is said the great orator used to pace backwards and forwards when composing his famous discourses, like another celebrated French writer, Balzac, wholly secluding himself from the world whilst thus occupied. A little garden-house in which he ate and slept leads out of this delightful walk, a cloister of greenery, the high square-cut walls of yew shutting out everything but the sky. What would some of us give for such a retreat as this! an ideal of perfect tranquillity and isolation from the outer world that might have satisfied the soul of Schopenhauer himself.

But the good things of life are not equally divided. The present Bishop, an octogenarian, who has long been quite blind, would perhaps prefer to hear more echoes from without. It happened that in one party was a little child of six, who, with the inquisitiveness of childhood, followed the servant in-doors, whilst the rest waited at the door for permission to visit the palace. "I hear the footsteps of a child" said the old man, and bidding his young visitor approach, he gave him sugar-plums, kisses, and finally his blessing. Very likely the innocent prattling of the child was as welcome to the old man as the sweetmeats to the little one on his knee.

The terraces of the Episcopal garden cross the ancient walls of the city, and underneath the boulevards afford a promenade almost as pleasant. It must be admitted that much more pains are taken in France to embellish provincial towns with shady walks and promenades than in England. The tiniest little town in Seine et Marne has its promenades, that is to say, an open green space and avenues with benches for the convenience of passers-by. We cannot, certainly, sit out of doors as much as our French neighbours in consequence of our more changeable climate, but might not pleasant public squares and gardens, with bands playing gratuitously on certain evenings in the week in country towns, entice customers from the public-house? The traveller is shown the handsome private residences of rich Meldois, where in the second week of September, 1870, were lodged the Emperor of Germany, the Prince Frederick Charles, and Prince Bismarck. Meaux, if one of the most prosperous, is also one of the most liberal of French cities, and has been renowned for its charity from early times. In the thirteenth century there were no fewer than sixty Hotels-Dieu, as well as hospitals for lepers in the diocese, and at the present day it is true to its ancient traditions, being abundantly supplied with hospitals, &c.

Half-an-hour from Meaux by railway is the pretty little town of La Ferte-sous-Jouarre, coquettishly perched on the Marne, and not yet rendered unpoetic by the hum and bustle of commerce. Here, even more than at Meaux, the material well-being of all classes is especially striking. You see the women sitting in their little gardens at needle-work, the children trotting off to school, the men busied in their respective callings, but all as it should be, no poverty, no dirt, no drunkenness, no discontent; cheerfulness, cleanliness, and good clothes are evidently everybody's portion. Yet it is eminently a working population; there are no fashionable ladies in the streets, no nursery-maids with over-dressed charges on the public walks; the men wear blue blouses, the women cotton gowns, all belonging to one class, and have no need to envy any others.

Close to the railway-station is a little house, where I saw an instance of the comfort enjoyed by these unpretentious citizens of this thrifty little town. The landlord, a particularly intelligent and well-mannered person, was waiting upon his customers in a blue cotton coat, and the landlady was as busy as could be in the kitchen. Both were evidently accustomed to plenty of hard work, yet when she took me over the house in order to show her accommodation for tourists, I found their own rooms furnished with Parisian elegance. There were velvet sofas and chairs, white-lace curtains, polished floors, mirrors, hanging wardrobes, a sump-tuous little bassinette for baby, and adjoining, as charming a room for their elder daughter--a teacher in a day-school--as any heiress to a large fortune could desire. This love of good furniture and in-door comfort generally, seemed to me to speak much, not only for the taste, but the moral tone of the family. Evidently to these good people the home meant everything dearest to their hearts. You would not find extravagance in food or dress among them, or most likely any other but this: they work hard, they live frugally, but, when the day's toil is done, they like to have pretty things around them, and not only to repose but to enjoy.

La Ferte-sous-Jouarre is the seat of a large manufacture of millstones, which are exported to all parts of the world, and it is a very thriving little place. Large numbers of Germans are brought hither by commerce, and now live again among their French neighbours as peacefully as before the war. The attraction for tourists is, however, the twin-town of Jouarre, reached by a lovely drive of about an hour from the little town. Leaving the river, you ascend gradually, gaining at every step a richer and wider prospect; below the blue river, winding between green banks, above a lofty ridge of wooded hill, with hamlets dotted here and there amid the yellow corn and luxuriant foliage. It is a bit of Switzerland, and has often been painted by French artists. I can fancy no more attractive field for a landscape-painter than this, who, provided he could endure the perpetual noise of the stone-yards, would find no lack of creature comforts.

The love of flowers and flower-gardens, so painfully absent in the West of France, is here conspicuous. There are flowers everywhere, and some of the little gardens give evidence of great skill and care. Jouarre is perched upon an airy green eminence, a quiet old-world town, with an enormous convent in the centre, where some scores of cloistered nuns have shut themselves up for the glory of God. There they live, these Bernardines, as they are called, as much in prison as if they were the most dangerous felons ever brought to justice; and a prison-house, indeed, the convent looks with its high walls, bars, and bolts. I had a little talk with the sister in charge of the porter's lodge, and she took me into the church, pointing to the high iron rails barring off the cloistered nuns, with that imbecile self-satisfaction as much inseparable from her calling as her unwholesome dress.

"There is one young English lady here," she said, "formerly a Protestant; she is twenty-one, and only the other day took the perpetual vows."

I wondered, as I looked up at the barred windows, how long this kind of Suttee would be permitted in happy France, or, indeed, in any other country, and whether in the life-time of that foolish English girl the doors would be opened and she would be compelled to live and labour in the world like any other rational being. This dreary prison-house, erected not in the interests of justice and society, but in order to pacify cupidity on one side and fanaticism on the other, afforded a painful contrast to the cheerful, active life outside.

Close to the convent is one of the most curious monuments in the entire department of Seine et Marne, namely, the famous Merovingian Crypt, described by French archaeologists in the "Bulletin Monumental" and elsewhere. It is well known that during the Merovingian epoch, and under Charlemagne, long journeys were often undertaken in order to procure marbles and other building materials for the Christian churches. Thus only can we account for the splendid columns of jasper, porphyry, and other rare marbles of which this crypt is composed. The capitals of white marble, in striking contrast to the deep reds, greens, and other colours of the columns, are richly carved with acanthus leaves, scrolls, and other classic patterns, without doubt the whole having originally decorated some Pagan temple. The chapel containing the crypt is said to have been founded in the seventh century, and speaks much for the enthusiasm and artistic spirit animating its builders. There is considerable elegance in these arches, also in the sculptured tombs of different epochs, which, like the crypt, have been preserved so wonderfully until the present time. Other archaeological treasures are here, notably the so-called "Pierre des Sonneurs de Jouarre," or Stone of the Jouarre Bell-ringers, a quaint design representing two bell-ringers at their task, with a legend underneath, dating from the fourteenth century.

It must be mentioned that the traveller's patience may undergo a trial here. When I arrived at Jouarre, M. le Cure and the sacristan were both absent, and as no one else possessed the key of the crypt, my chance of seeing it seemed small. However, some one obligingly set out on a voyage of discovery, and finally the sacristan's wife was found in a neighbouring harvest-field, and she bustled up, delighted to show everything; amongst other antiquities some precious skulls and bones of Saints are kept under lock and key in the sacristy, and only exposed on fete days.

In the middle ages, Jouarre possessed an important abbey, which was destroyed during the Great Revolution. There are also in a lovely little island, in the river close to the town, remains of a feudal castle where Louis XVI. and Marie Antoinette halted on their way to Paris after their capture at Varennes. No one, however, need to have archaeological tastes in order to visit these little towns; alike scenery and people are charming, and the tourist is welcomed as a guest rather than a customer. But whether at Jouarre, or anywhere else, he who knows most will see most, every day the dictum of the great Lessing being illustrated in travel: "Wer viel weisst hat viel zu sorgen--" "Who knows much has much to look after." The mere lover of the picturesque, who cares nothing for French history, literature, and institutions, old or new, will get a superb landscape here, and nothing more.

Our resting place at Couilly, where, sheltered by acacia trees, we hardly feel the tropical heat of July, is an admirable starting point for excursions, each interesting in a different way. The striking contrast with the homely ease and well to do terre-a-terre about us is the princely chateau of the Rothschilds at Ferrieres, which none should miss seeing on any account whatever. With princely liberality also, Baron Rothschild admits anyone to his fairy-land who takes the trouble to write for permission, and however much we may have been thinking of King Solomon, Haroun al Raschid, and the thousand and one nights, we shall not be disappointed. The very name of Rothschild fills us with awe and bewilderment! We prepare ourselves to be dazzled with gold and gems, to tread on carpets gorgeous as peacock's tails, softer than eider-down, to pass through jasper and porphyry columns into regal halls where the acme of splendour can go no farther, where the walls are hung with rich tapestries, where every chair looks like a throne, and where on all sides mirrors reflect the treasures collected from different parts of the world, and we are not disappointed.

Quitting the railway at the cheerful and wealthy little town of Lagny, we drive past handsome country-houses, and well-kept flower-gardens, then gradually ascend a road winding amid hill and valley to the chateau, a graceful structure in white marble, or so it seems, proudly commanding the wide landscape. The flower-gardens are a blaze of colours, and the orange trees give delicious fragrance as we ascend the terrace, ascend being hardly the word applicable to steps sloping so easily upwards, so nicely adjusted to the human foot that climbing Mont Blanc, under the same circumstances, would be accomplished without fatigue. It is impossible to give any idea of the different kinds of magnificence that greet us on every side, now a little Watteau-like boudoir, having for background sky-blue satin and roses; now a dining-hall, sombre, gorgeous, and majestic as that of a Spanish palace; now we are transported to Persia, China, and Japan, the next we find ourselves amid unspeakable treasures of Italian and other marbles.

To come down to practical details, it might be suggested to the generous owner of this noble treasure-home of art that the briefest possible catalogue of his choicest treasures would unspeakably oblige his visitors. There is hardly a piece of furniture that is not interesting, alike from an historic and artistic point of view, whilst some are chefs-d'oeuvre both in design and execution, and dazzlingly rich in material. Among these may be mentioned a pair of chimney ornaments, thickly hung with pendants of precious stones, a piano--which belonged to Marie Antoinette--the case of which is formed of tortoiseshell, richly decorated with gold; an inlaid cabinet, set with emeralds, sapphires, and other jewels; another composed of precious stones; chairs and couches crowned with exquisite tapestry of the Louis Quinze period; some rare specimens of old cloisonne work, also of Florentine mosaics--these forming a small part of this magnificent museum.

The striking feature is the great quantity and variety of rich marbles in every part. One of the staircases is entirely formed of different kinds of rare marble, the effect being extra-ordinarily imposing. Elsewhere, a room is divided by Corinthian columns of jasper and porphyry, and on every side are displayed a wealth and splendour in this respect quite unique. Without doubt, nothing lends such magnificence to interiors as marbles, but they require the spaciousness and princeliness of such a chateau to be displayed to advantage.

Next in importance, as a matter of mere decoration, must be cited the tapestries of which there is a rare and valuable collection, chiefly in the hall, so called, where they are arrayed about the running gallery surmounting the pictures. What this hall must be worth would perhaps sound fabulous on paper, but it is here that some of the most precious treasures are found; cabinets of ivory, ebony, gems, gold, and silver, and the pictures alone represent a princess's dowry. Examples of some of the greatest masters are here: Velasquez, Rembrandt, Rubens, Claude Lorraine, the Caracci, Bordone, Reynolds, lastly among moderns, Ingres and Hippolyte Flandrin. Much might be said about these pictures, if space permitted, but they alone are worth making the journey from Paris or Couilly to see.

We find a very pleasing Murillo and some exquisite little specimens of the early German school in other parts of the chateau, although the gems of the collection are undoubtedly the Bordones, Rembrandts, and Reynoldses. But the creme de la creme of Baron Rothschild's treasures is not to be found in this sumptuous hall, in spite of tapestries, pictures, marbles and rare furniture, nor in the state salon, but in the dining-room, a marvellously rich and gorgeous apartment, where the wealth of gold and splendid colours is toned down, and the eye is rather refreshed than dazzled by the whole. On the walls, reaching from base to ceiling, are hung a series of paintings on leather, known as the Cuirs de Cordoue, leather paintings of Cordova. They are historic and allegorical subjects, and are painted in rich colours with a great abundance of gold on a dark background, the general effect being that of a study in gold and brown.

As good luck would have it, immediately after my visit to Ferrieres, I happened to hear of the Baron Davillier's learned little treatise on this ancient leather-work, or Guadamaciles, variously called cuir d'or, cuirs dores, cuirs basanes, &c. The history of these artistic varieties is so curious, that I will give it in as few words as possible.

Guadamacil, a Spanish word, signifying painted leather, is supposed to have its origin in the city of Ghadames, Sahara, where M. Duveyrier the eminent French explorer, was making scientific inquiries in 1860. The Kadi knowing M. Duveyrier's interest in all that concerned the history of this city in the desert, drew his attention to the following passage in the geographical work of a learned Tunisian, dating from the sixth century of the Hegira, that is to say, the twelfth of our era. "Ghadames--from this city come the painted leathers or Ghadamesien." M. Duveyrier accepted this etymology of the word as the most natural, seeing that the Moors of Spain, and especially of Cordova, had constant intercourse with the inhabitants of North Africa, and would naturally receive these with other artistic curiosities. The Arab dictionary of Freytag confirms M. Duveyrier's etymology, the author thus describing Ghadames--"Nomen oppidi in Africa, unde pelles gudsamiticae appellatae sunt."

Whatever its origin, we find the fabrication of these guadamaciles very flourishing at Cordova in the sixteenth century. The preparation of sheep and goat-skins for artistic purposes was a source of considerable commercial wealth to this city, and they were largely exported to various parts of Europe and India. A writer of that period describes the glowing effect of the Cordovan streets tapestried with the richly gilt and painted skins hung out to dry before packing; whilst Cervantes is supposed to have one in his mind, when thus describing the heroine of one of his plays, "Enter Hortigosa, wearing a guadamacile, &c." Rabelais also alludes to the subject in Pantagruel:--"De la peau de ces moutons seront faictes les beaux maroquins, lesquels on vendra pour maroquins Turquins ou de Montelimart, ou de Hespaigne."

The guadamaciles, although leather-work was fabricated in several cities of France, also of Italy and Belgium, ever remained a speciality of Spain, Seville, Barcelona, Lerida, Ciudad-Real, and Valladolid bearing the palm after Cordova. Such works are characterized by elaborateness, splendour of colour and richness of detail. The curious may consult the Recherches sur le Cuir dore, anciennement appele Cuir basane, by M. de la Queriere, also M. Jacquemart's Histoire du Mobilier, in which is found a very exact representation of a specimen, probably Italian. The art decayed in Spain after the expulsion of the Moors in 1610, but was introduced in various parts of France by some of the exiled artists, and it may be said to have died out in France about the end of the last century.

Senor Riano's handbook to the Spanish collection in the South Kensington Museum gives a list with details of the specimens there exhibited, numbering upwards of twenty panels and borders for furniture. These are chiefly seventeenth century work-tables, exceedingly interesting and valuable. All lovers of art, furniture, and decoration generally can but echo M. Davilliers' hope that the art of painting and stamping on leather may be ere long revived at Cordova.

So much for the artistic treat in store for those art-lovers who find their way to the Chateau of Ferrieres, where none will fail to add to his previous stock of knowledge. Art-lovers cannot study the exquisite design, elaborate workmanship, and splendid materials of the furniture, decoration, and general fittings up of such a palace without some sadness. How little that is new and modern can here be compared with the old, whether we regard mere carpentry detail or solidity! This is strikingly illustrated in the Japanese cloisonne work of which there are some choice specimens.

Two refinements of civilization will amuse the stranger; the first is a railway in miniature from kitchens to dining-rooms, by means of which the dishes are conveyed to the latter with the utmost possible dispatch. The temper indeed of these happy diners should be ineffably serene, considering that they can never be ruffled by soups or fish coming to table one degree less hot than the most epicurean palate could desire. Luxury can go no farther, unless, which may be invented some day, a patent appetite and digesting apparatus were supplied, enabling host and guests to sit down every day to the feasts spread before them with undiminished relish and perfect impunity.

The second amusing, or rather surprising, fact is that of the luxurious, though I venture to say somewhat floridly decorated ladies smoking room? Were we dreaming? Or was it our informant who was but half awake or in error? I believe not, and that the elegant and princely Chateau de Ferrieres thus acknowledges the fact of lady smokers!

CHAPTER II.
NOISIEL: THE CITY OF CHOCOLATE.

When not disposed to go far a-field in search of pleasure or instruction, we find plenty to interest us close at hand. Even in this quiet little village there is always something going on, a fete patronale, a ball, a prize-distribution, or other local event. The Ecole Communale for both boys and girls has just closed for the holidays, so last Sunday--the season in July--the prizes were given away with much ceremony. A tent was decorated with tricolour flags, evergreens, and garlands, the village band escorted thither the Mayor and Corporation, marching them in with a spirited air, the entire community having turned out to see. I had already witnessed a prize-distribution in the heart of Anjou, but how different from this! Here at Couilly it was difficult to believe that the fashionable Parisian toilettes around us belonged to the wives of small farmers, who all the week were busy in their dairies, whilst the young ladies of all ages, from five to fifteen, their daughters, might have appeared at the Lady Mayoress's ball at Guildhall, so smart were they in their white muslin frocks and blue and pink sashes and hair-knots. A few mob-caps among the old women and blue blouses among the men were seen, but the assemblage, as a whole, might be called a fashionable one--whilst at Anjou, exactly the same class presented the homeliest appearance, all the female part of it wearing white coiffes and plain stuff gowns, the men blue blouses and sabots. Nor was the difference less striking in other respects. These sons and daughters of rich tenant-farmers, peasant proprietors, or even day-labourers, are far ahead of the young people in Anjou, and each would be considered a wonder in benighted Brittany. They are, in fact, quite accomplished, not only learning singing, drawing and other accomplishments, but are able to take part in dramatic entertainments. Two performances were given by the boys, two by the girls, a little play being followed by a recitation; and I must say I never heard anything of the kind in a village-school in England.

These children acquitted themselves of their parts remarkably well, especially the girls, and their accuracy, pure accent, and delivery generally, spoke volumes for the training they had received; of awkwardness there was not a trace. Of course there were speeches from the Mayor, M. le Cure, and others, also music and singing, and a large number of excellent books were distributed, each recipient being at the same time crowned with a wreath of artificial flowers.

It is to be hoped that ere many years, thanks to the new law enforcing compulsory education, the excellent education these children receive will be the portion of every boy and girl in France, and that an adult unable to read and write--the rule, not the exception, among the rural population in Brittany--will be unheard of. A friend of mine from Nantes recently took with her to Paris a young Breton maid-servant, who had been educated by the "Bonnes Soeurs," that is to say the nuns. What was the poor girl's astonishment to find that in Paris everybody was so far accomplished as to be able to read and write? Her surprise would have been greater still, had she witnessed the acquirements of these little Couilly girls, many of them, like herself, daughters of small peasant farmers.

It must be mentioned, for the satisfaction of those who regard the progress of education with some concern, that the elegant bonnets and dresses I speak of are laid aside on week days, and that nowhere in France do people work harder than here. But when not at work they like to wear good clothes and read the newspapers as well as their neighbours. Take our laundress, for instance, an admirable young woman, who gets up clothes to perfection, and who on Sunday exchanges her cotton gown and apron for the smartest of Parisian costumes. The amount of underclothes these countrywomen possess is sometimes enormous, and they pride themselves upon the largest possible quantity, a great part of which is of course laid by. They count their garments not by dozens but by scores, and can thus afford to wait for the quarterly washing-day, as they often do. It must be also mentioned that cleanliness is uniformly found throughout these flourishing villages, and, in most, hot and cold public baths. Dirt is rare--I might almost say unknown--also rags, neither of which as yet we have seen throughout our long walks and drives, except in the case of a company of tramps we encountered one day. Drunkenness is also comparatively absent, in some places we might say absolutely.

As we make further acquaintance with these favoured regions, we might suppose that here, at least, the dreams of Utopians had come true, and that poverty, squalor, and wretchedness were banished for ever. The abundant crops around us are apportioned out to all, and the soil, which, if roughly cultivated according to English notions, yet bears marvellously, is not the heritage of one or two, but of the people. The poorest has his bit of land, to which he adds from time to time by the fruit of his industry, and though tenant-farming is carried on largely, owing to the wealth and enterprize of the agricultural population, the tenant-farmers almost always possess land of their own, and they hire more in order to save money for future purchases. Of course they could only make tenant-farming pay by means of excessive economy and laboriousness, as the rents are high, but in these respects they are not wanting.

The fertility of the soil is not more astonishing than the variety of produce we find here, though pasturage and cheese-making are their chief occupations, and fruit crops are produced in other parts. We find, as has been before mentioned, fruit-trees everywhere, corn, fruit, and vegetables all growing with unimaginable luxuriance. The pastures are also very fine, but we see no cattle out to graze; the harvest work requires all hands, and, as there are no fences between field and meadow, there is no one to tend them. The large heap of manure being dried up by the sun in the midst of the farm-yard, has a look of unthriftiness, whilst the small, dark, and ill-ventilated dairies make us wonder that the manufacture of the famous Brie cheese should be the profitable thing it is. At one farm we visited, we saw thirty-six splendid Normandy cows, the entire milk produce of which was used for cheese-making. Yet nothing could be worse than the dairy arrangements from a hygienic point of view, and the absolute cleanliness requisite for dairy work was wanting. These Brie cheeses are made in every farm, small or great, and large quantities are sent to the Meaux market on Saturdays, where the sale alone reaches the sum of five or six millions of francs yearly. The process is a very simple one, and is of course perpetually going on.

Our hostess, at one of the larger and more prosperous of these farms, showed us everything, and regaled us abundantly with the fresh milk warm from the cow. Here we saw an instance of the social metamorphosis taking place in these progressive districts. The mistress of the house, a bright clever woman, occupied all day with the drudgery of the farm-house, is fairly educated; and, though now neatly dressed in plain cotton gown, on Sunday dresses like any other lady for the promenade. Her mother, still clinging to the past custom, appeared in short stuff petticoat, wooden shoes, and yellow-handkerchief wrapped round her head; while the children, who, in due time, will be trained to toil like their neighbours, are now being well taught in the village school.

These people are wealthy, and may be taken as types of the farming class here, though many of the so called cultivateurs, or proprietors, farming their own land, live in much easier style; the men managing the business, the ladies keeping the house, and the work of the farm being left to labourers. The rent of good land is about fifty shillings an acre, and wages, in harvest time, four francs with board. The farms, while large in comparison with anything found in Brittany and Anjou, are small, measured by our scale, being from fifty to two or three hundred acres.

Steam-threshing has long been in use here; but, of course, not generally, as the smaller patches of corn only admit of the old system; and the corn is so ripe that it is often threshed on the field immediately after the cutting; the harvesting process is rapid; we often see only one or two labourers, whether men or women, on a single patch. But there is no waiting, as a rule, for fine weather to cart away the corn, and masters and men work with a will. We must, indeed, watch a harvest from beginning to end to realise the laboriousness of a farmer's life here. Upon one occasion, when visiting a farm of a hundred and thirty acres, we found the farmer and his mother, rich people, both hard at work in the field, the former casting away straw--the corn being threshed by machinery on the field--the latter tying it up.

The look of cheerfulness animating all faces was delightful to behold. The farmer's countenance beamed with satisfaction, and, one may be sure, not without good cause. The farmhouse and buildings are spacious and handsome, and, as is generally the case here, were surrounded by a high wall, having a large court in the centre, where a goodly number of geese, turkeys, and poultry were disporting themselves. There we found only a few cows, but they were evidently very productive from the quantity of cheeses found in the dairy.[1]

1   The curious in agriculture never need fear to ask a question or two of these flourishing farmers and farmeresses of Seine et Marne. Busy as they are, they are never too busy to be courteous, and are always ready to show any part of the premises to strangers.

Sheep are not kept here largely, and grazing bullocks still less. The farmer, therefore, relies chiefly on his dairy, next on his corn and fruit crops, and, as bad seasons are rare, both these seldom fail him. But these pleasant villages have generally some other interest besides their rich harvest and picturesque sites. In some of the smallest, you may find exquisite little churches, such as La Chapelle-sur-Crecy, a veritable cathedral in miniature. Crecy was once an important place with ninety-nine towers and double ramparts, traces of which still remain.

A narrow stream runs at the back of the town, and quaint enough are the little houses perched beside it, each with its garden and tiny drawbridge, drawn at night, the oddest sights of which a sketcher might make something. A sketcher, indeed, must be a happy person here, so many quiet subjects offering themselves at every turn. Many of these village churches date from the thirteenth century, and are alike picturesque within and without, their spires and gabled towers giving these leading characters to the landscape. Nowhere in France do you find prettier village churches, not a few ranking among the historic monuments of the country. Here and there are chateaux with old-fashioned gardens and noble avenues, and we have only to ask permission at the porter's lodge, to walk in and enjoy them at leisure.

In one of these the lady of the house, who was sitting out of doors, kindly beckoned us to enter, and we had the pleasure of listening, under some splendid oaks, to the oriole's song, and of seeing a little cluster of Eucalyptus trees, two surprises we had not looked for. The oriole, a well known and beautiful American bird, also a songster that may be compared to the nightingale, is indeed no stranger here, and, having once heard and seen him, you cannot mistake him for any other bird. His song is an invariable prognostic of rain, as we discover on further acquaintance.

The Eucalyptus Globulus, or blue gum tree, a native of Australia, and now so successfully acclimatized in Algeria, the Cape, the Riviera, and other countries, is said to flourish in the region of the olive only; but we were assured by the lady of the house that it bears the frost of these northern regions. I confess I thought her plantations looked rather sickly, and considering that the climate is like that of Paris, subject to short spells of severe cold in winter and sudden changes, I doubt much in the experiment. But the health-giving, fever-destroying Eucalyptus is not needed in this well-wooded healthy country, and the splendid foliage of acacia, walnut, oaks, and birch leaves nothing to desire either in the matter of shade or ornament.

A lover of trees, birds, and whispering breezes will say that here at least is a corner of the Happy Fields of Homer, or the Islands of the Blest described by Hesiod.

Nowhere is summer to be more revelled in, more amply tasted, than in these rustic villages, where creature comforts yet abound, and nowhere is the dolce far niente so easily induced. Why should we be at the trouble of undertaking a hot, dusty railway journey in search of Gaelic tombs, Gothic churches, or Merovingian remains when we have the essence of deliciousness at our very door?--waving fields of ripe corn, amid which the reapers in twos and threes are at work--picturesque figures that seemed to have walked out of Millet's canvas--lines of poplars along the curling river, beyond hills covered with woods, a clustering village, or a chateau, here and there. This is the picture, partially screened by noble acacia trees, that I have from my window, accompanied by the music of waving barley and wheat, dancing leaves, and chaffinches, tame as canaries, singing in the branches.

About a mile off is the little village of Villiers, which is even prettier than our own, and which of course artists have long ago found out. The wayside inn near the bridge, crossing the little river Morin, bears witness to the artistic popularity of this quiet spot. The panels of the parlour are covered with sketches, some in oil, some in water-colour, souvenirs with which visitors have memorialized their stay. Some of these hasty effects are very good, and the general effect is heightened by choice old pottery, tastefully arranged above. Villiers-sur-Morin would be an admirable summer resort for an artist fond of hanging woods, running streams, and green pastures, and a dozen more possessing the same attraction lie close at hand.

But, though within so easy a distance of Paris, life is homely, and fastidious travellers must keep to the beaten tracks and high roads where good hotels are to be found. When he goes into the by-ways, a way-side inn is all that he must expect, and, if there is no diligence, a lift in the miller's or baker's cart; the farmers' wives driving to market with their cheese and butter are always willing to give the stranger a seat, but money must not be offered in return for such obligingness. We must never forget that, if these country folks are laborious, and perhaps sordid, in their thriftiness, they are proud, and refuse to be paid for what costs them nothing. The same characteristic is very generally found in France.

Fishing is the principal amusement here, and shared by both sexes. What the Marne and the Morin contain in the way of booty, we hardly know; but it is certain that more cunning fish, whether perch, tench, or bream, never existed, and are not, "by hook or by crook," to be caught. Wherever we go, we find anglers sitting patiently by these lovely green banks, and certainly the mere prospect they have before them--clear water reflecting water-mill and lofty poplar trees and shelving banks now a tangle of wild flowers--is enough to make such indolence agreeable. But, after days and days of fruitless waiting for the prey that always eludes them, we do wonder at such persistence. Is nothing then ever caught in these pleasant streams, will ask the inquiring reader? Well, yes, I have seen served at table perch the size of very small herrings, which it is the French fashion to take between the fingers daintily, and, holding by head and tail, nibble as children bite an apple. Whether indeed these little fish are caught by the angler, I know not; but this is certainly the way they are eaten--if inelegant, honi soit qui mal y pense.

Next to fishing, the favourite pastime here is swimming, also indulged in largely by the gentler sex. The pedestrian, in his ramble along winding river and canal, will be sure to surprise a group of water-nymphs sporting in the water, their bathing costumes being considered quite a sufficient guarantee against ill-natured comment. The men are more careless of appearance, and, if they can get a good bathing place tolerably hidden from the world, take their bath or swim in nature's dress. In all these river-side towns and villages are public baths, swimming schools, and doubtless the prevailing love of water in these parts may partly account for the healthful looks and fine physiques of the population. In fact, people are as clean here as they are the reverse in Brittany, and the blue linen clothes, invariably worn by the men, are constantly in the wash, and are as cool, comfortable and cleanly as it is possible to conceive. English folks have yet to learn how to dress themselves healthfully and appropriately in hot weather, and here they might take a hint.

But no matter how enamoured of green fields and woodland walks, we must tear ourselves away for a day to see the famous "Chocolate city" of M. Menier, the modern marvel par excellence of the county, and, as a piece of the most perfect organization it is possible to conceive, one of the wonders of the world. M. Menier has undoubtedly arrived at making the best chocolate that ever rejoiced the palate; he has achieved far greater things than this, in giving us one of the happiest and most delightful social pictures that ever charmed the heart. Such things must be seen to be realized, but I will as briefly as possible give an account of what I saw.

Again, we make the pretty little town of Lagny our starting point, and, having passed a succession of scattered farm-houses and wide corn-fields, we come gradually upon a miniature town, built in red and white; so coquettishly, airily, daintily placed is the City of Chocolate amid orchards and gardens, that, at first sight, a spectator is inclined to take it rather for a settlement of such dreamers as assembled together at Brook Farm to poetize, philosophize, and make love, than of artizans engaged in the practical business of life. This long street of charming cottages, having gardens around and on either side, is planted with trees, so that in a few years' time it will form as pleasant a promenade as the Parisian boulevards. We pass along, admiring the abundance of flowers everywhere, and finally reach a large open square around which are a congeries of handsome buildings, all like the dwelling houses, new, cheerful, and having trees and benches in front. This is the heart of the "Cite," to be described by-and-by, consisting of Co-operative Stores, Schools, Libraries, &c.; beyond, stands the chateau of M. Menier, surrounded by gardens, and before us the manufactory. The air is here fragrant, not with roses and jessamine, but with the grateful aroma of chocolate, reminding us that we are indeed in a city, if not literally a pile, of cocoa, yet owing its origin to the products of that wonderful tree, or rather to the ingenuity by which its resources have been turned to such account.

The works are built on the river Marne, and, having seen two vast hydraulic machines, we enter a lift with the intelligent foreman deputed to act as guide, and ascend to the topmost top of the many storied, enormous building in which the cocoa berry is metamorphosed into the delicious compound known as Chocolate Menier. This is a curious experience, and the reverse of most other intellectual processes, since here, instead of mounting the ladder of knowledge gradually, we find ourselves placed on a pinnacle of ignorance, from which we descend by degrees, finding ourselves enlightened when we at last touch the ground.

Our aerial voyage accomplished, we see process the first, namely, the baking of the berry, this, of course, occupying a vast number of hands, all men, on account of the heat and laboriousness required in the operation. Descending a story, we find the cocoa berry already in a fair way to become edible, and giving out an odour something like chocolate; here the process consists in sorting and preparing the vast masses of cocoa for grinding. Lower still, we find M. Menier's great adjunct in the fabrication of chocolate, namely, sugar, coming into play, and no sooner are sugar and cocoa put together than the compound becomes chocolate in reality. Lower still, we find processes of refining and drying going on, an infinite number being required before the necessary firmness is attained. Lower still, we come to a very hot place indeed, but, like all the other vast compartments of the manufactory, as well ventilated, spacious, and airy as is possible to conceive, the workman's inconvenience from the heat being thereby reduced to a minimum.

Here it is highly amusing to watch the apparently intelligent machines which divide the chocolate into half-pound lumps, the process being accomplished with incredible swiftness. Huge masses of chocolate in this stage awaiting the final preparation are seen here and there, all destined at last to be put half a pound at a time into a little baking tin, and to be baked like a hot cross bun, the name of Menier being stamped on at the same time. A good deal of manipulation is necessary in this process; but we must go down a stage lower to see the dexterity and swiftness with which the chief manual tasks in the fabrication of chocolate are performed.

Here women are chiefly employed, and their occupation is to envelope the half-pound cakes of chocolate in three papers, first silver, next white, and finally sealing it up in the well-known yellow cover familiar to all of us. These feminine fingers work so fast, and with such marvellous precision, that, if the intricate pieces of machinery we have just witnessed seemed gifted with human intelligence and docility, on the other hand the women at work in this department appeared like animated machines; no blundering, no halting, no alteration of working pace. Their fluttering fingers, indeed, worked with beautiful promptitude and regularity, and as everybody in M. Menier's City of Chocolate is well-dressed and cheerful, there was nothing painful in the monotony of their toil or unremitting application.

On the same floor are the packing departments, where we see the cases destined for all parts of the world.

Thus quickly and easily we have descended the ladder of learning, and have acquired some faint notion of the way in which the hard, brown, tasteless cocoa berry is transformed into one of the most agreeable and wholesome compounds as yet invented for our delectation. Of course, many intermediate processes have had to be passed by, also many interesting features in the organization of the various departments; these, to be realized, must be seen.

There are one or two points, however, I will mention. In the first place, when we consider the enormous duty on sugar, and the fact that chocolate, like jam, is composed half of sugar and half of berry, we are at first at a loss to understand how chocolate-making can bring in such large returns as it must do--in the first place, to have made M. Menier a millionaire, in the second, to enable him to carry out his philanthropic schemes utterly regardless of cost. But we must remember that there is but one Chocolate Menier in the world, and that in spite of the enormous machinery at work, night and day, working day and Sunday, supply can barely keep pace with demand. A staff of night-workers are always at rest in the day-time, in order to keep the machinery going at work, and, to my regret, I learned that the work-shops are not closed on Sundays. M. Menier's work-people doubtless get ample holidays, but the one day's complete rest out of the seven, the portion of all with us, is denied them. By far the larger portion of the Chocolate Menier is consumed in France, where, as in England and America, it stands unrivalled. M. Menier may therefore be said to possess a monopoly, and, seeing how largely he lavishes his ample wealth on others, none can grudge him such good fortune.

Having witnessed the transformation of one of the most unpromising looking berries imaginable into the choicest of sweetmeats, the richest of the cups "that cheer but not inebriate;" lastly, one of the best and most nourishing of the lighter kinds of food--we have to witness a transformation more magical still, namely, the hard life of toil made easy, the drudgery of mechanical labour lightened, the existence of the human machine made hopeful, healthful, reasonable, and happy. Want, squalor, disease, and drunkenness have been banished from the City of Chocolate, and thrift, health, and prosperity reign in their stead.

Last of all, ignorance has vanished also, a thorough education being the happy portion of every child born within its precincts. Our first visit was to what is called the "Ecole Gardienne," or infant school--like the rest kept up entirely at M. Menier's expense--and herein, the grandest gift of organization is seen, perhaps, more strikingly than anywhere. These children, little trotting things from three to five years old, have a large playground, open in summer and covered in winter, and a spacious school-room, in which they receive little lessons in singing, A B C, and so on. Instead of being perched on high benches without backs, and their legs dangling, as is the case in convent schools for the poor, they have delightful little low easy-chairs and tables accommodated to their size, each little wooden chair, with backs, having seats for two, so that, instead of being crowded and disturbing each other, the children sit in couples with plenty of room and air, and in perfect physical comfort. No hollow chests, no bent backs, no crookedness here. Happy and comfortable as princes these children sit in their chairs, having their feet on the floor, and their backs where they ought to be, namely, as a support.

Leading out of the school-room are two small rooms, where we saw a pleasant sight; a dozen cots, clean and cosy as it is possible to conceive, on which rosy, sturdy boys and girls of a year old were taking their midday sleep. We next went into the girls' school, which is under the charge of a certificated mistress, and where children remain till thirteen or fourteen years of age, receiving exactly the same education as the boys, and without a fraction of cost to the parents. The course of study embraces all branches of elementary knowledge, with needlework, drawing, history, singing and book-keeping. Examinations are held and certificates of progress awarded. We found the girls taking a lesson in needle-work--the only point in which their education differs from that of the boys--and the boys at their drawing class; the school-rooms are lofty, well-aired, and admirably arranged.

Adjoining the schools is the library, open to all members of the community, and where many helps to adult study are afforded. On the other side of the pleasant green square, so invitingly planted with trees, stand the Cooperative Stores, which are, of course, an important feature in the organization of the community. Here meat, groceries, and other articles of daily domestic consumption are sold at low prices, and of the best possible quality: the membership, of course, being the privilege of the thrifty and the self-denying, who belong to the Association by payment. I did not ask if intoxicating drinks were sold on the premises, for such an inquiry would have been gratuitous. The cheerful, tidy, healthful looks of the population proclaimed their sobriety, and some excellent sirop de groseille offered me in the cottage of the foreman who acted as guide, showed that such delicious drinks are made at home as to necessitate no purchases abroad.

There is also a Savings' Bank, which all are invited to patronize; six and a half per cent being the incentive held out to those economisers on a small scale. But neither the school, nor the Co-operative Store, nor the Savings' Bank can make the working man's life what it should be without the home, and it is with the home that alike M. Menier's philanthropy and organization attain the acme. These dwellings, each block containing two, are admirably arranged, with two rooms on the ground-floor, two above, a capital cellar and office, and last, but not least, a garden. The workman pays a hundred and twenty francs, rather less than five pounds, a year for this accommodation, which it is hardly necessary to say is the portion of very few artizans in France, or elsewhere. The Cite, as it is called, being close to the works, they can go home to meals, and, though the women are largely employed in the manufactory, the home need not be neglected. It was delightful to witness my cicerone's pleasure in his home. He was a workman of superior order, and though, as he informed me, of no great education, yet possessed of literary and artistic tastes. The little parlour was as comfortable a room as any reasonable person could desire. There were books on the shelves, and pictures over the mantelpiece. Among these, were portraits of Thiers, Gambetta, and M. Menier, for all of whom their owner expressed great admiration.

"Ah!" he said, "I read the newspaper and I know a little history, but in my time education was not thought of. These children here have now the chance of being whatever they like."

He showed me his garden, every inch of which was made use of--fruit, flowers, and vegetables growing luxuriantly on this well-selected site. The abundance of flowers was particularly striking, especially to those familiar with certain districts in France, where the luxury of a flower is never indulged in; M. Menier himself must have as strong a passion for gardening as for philanthropy, judging from the enormous gardens adjoining his handsome chateau, and perhaps his love of flowers--always a most humanizing taste--has set the example. These brilliant parterres, whether seen in the vast domains of the master or the humble homesteads of the men, delightfully break the red and white uniformity of the City of Chocolate, flowers above, around, on every side. There is also a profusion of fruit and vegetables, land quite recently laid under cultivation soon yielding returns in this favoured spot.

Before quitting Noisiel we must remark that M. Menier possesses cocoa and sugar plantations in the Southern States of America, and is thus enabled to fabricate the best possible chocolate at the lowest possible price. The cocoa-berry, sugar, and essence of vanilla alone form the ingredients of this delicious compound, which for the most part is made of one quality only. The amount of water power used daily, the quantity of material consumed and chocolate manufactured, the entire consumption throughout France, all these are interesting statistics, and are found elsewhere--my object being a graphic description of M. Menier's "Chocolaterie", and nothing further. The interest to general readers and writers consists not so much in such facts as these as in the astonishing completeness of the manufactory as a piece of organization, and the great social and moral well-being of which it is made the channel. Something more than mere business talent and philanthropy is necessary to combine the material and moral forces we find at work here. M. Menier must have gone into every practical detail, not only of hygiene and domestic economy, but of education, to have put into working order so admirable a scheme as his; and by living among his work-people he is enabled to watch the result of his efforts. The handsome chateau, with its magnificent garden in close proximity to the "Cite", preaches a daily text, which we may be sure is more effective than any amount of words. By his own capacity and exertions M. Menier has realized the splendid fortune he now uses so philanthropically, and equally by this same capacity and exertion only can his working men lift themselves in the social scale. The children educated at Noisiel will have their fortune in their own hands, since in France fortune and the highest social distinctions are within reach of all; and, in thus educating her future citizens, the great chocolate manufacturer is fulfilling the part not only of a philanthropist but of a true patriot.

The French nation now recognise the fact, long since evident to outsiders, that the last great contest between France and Germany was a struggle less between two vast armed forces than between instruction and alertness on the one hand, and ignorance and indolence on the other. Now that French youth is urged and compelled to put its shoulder to the wheel, and duty before pleasure, none can despair of the future of France. Wherever I go, in whatever corner of the world I henceforth taste the renowned Chocolate Menier, I shall be reminded of something which will lend additional sweetness and flavour to it. I shall recall a community of working people whose toil is lightened and elevated, whose daily portion is made hopeful, reasonable, and happy, by an ever-active sympathy and benevolence rarely found allied. More lessons than one will be carried away by the least and most instructed visitor of the flourishing little City of Chocolate on the banks of the Marne.

Church-going in this rich country is at all times a dreary affair, but especially just now, when partly from the harvest work going on all Sunday, and partly from lack of devotion, both Catholic and Protestant places of worship are all but empty. For there is a strong Protestant element here, dating from the epoch of the Revocation of the Edict of Nantes, and in the neighbouring village of Quincey are a Protestant Church and school. One Sunday morning I set off with two friends to attend service in the latter, announced to take place at eleven o'clock, but on arriving found the "Temple" locked, and not a sign of any coming ceremonial. Being very hungry, after the long walk through cornfields and vineyards, I went to a little baker's shop in search of a roll, and there realized the hospitable spirit of these good Briards. The mistress of the shop very kindly invited me into a little back room, and regaled me with excellent household bread, Brie cheese, and the wine of the country, refusing to be paid for her refreshments.

This little meal finished, I rejoined my friends at the church, which was now open, and, in company of half a dozen school-children, we quietly waited to see what would eventually take place. By-and-by, one or two peasant-folks dropped in, picturesque old men and women, the latter in black and blue dresses and mob-caps. Then the schoolmaster appeared, and we were informed that it being the first Sunday in the month, the pastor had to do duty in an adjoining parish, according to custom, and that the schoolmaster would read the prayers and lessons instead. A psalm was sung, portions of Scripture and short prayers were read, another straggler or two joining the little congregation as the service went on. The schoolmaster, who officiated, played the harmonium and sang exceedingly well, finally read a brief exposition on the portion of Scripture read, whereupon after further singing we broke up.

It was pleasant to find that the children, who looked particularly intelligent, were in such good hands. These country pastors, like the priests, receive very small pay from the State. How these isolated communities can keep up their schools seems astonishing, and speaks well for the zeal animating the Protestant body in France. As all the schools are now closed in consequence of the harvest, we could not see the children at work.

In the afternoon I went to the parish church of Couilly, whilst vespers were going on. If the little Protestant assemblage I had just before witnessed was touching, this was almost painful, and might have afforded an artist an admirable subject for a picture. Sitting on a high stool, with his back to the congregation, consisting of three old women, was the priest, on either side the vergers, one in white stole, the other in purple robe and scarlet cap, all these chanting in loud monotonous tones, and of course in Latin, now and then the harmonium giving a faint accompaniment. On either side of these automatic figures were rows of little boys in scarlet and white, who from time to time made their voices heard also. As a background to this strange scene, was the loveliest little Gothic interior imaginable, the whiteness of aisle and transept being relieved by the saffron-coloured ribs of the arches and columns; the Church of Couilly being curious without and beautiful within, like many other parish churches here. After a time, one of the vergers blew out the three wax lights on a side altar, and all three retired, each scurrying away in different directions with very little show of reverence.

How different from the crowded churches in Brittany, where, whether at mass or vespers, hardly standing-room is to be found! How long Catholicism will hold its sway over the popular mind there depends, of course, greatly on the priests themselves, who, if ignorant and coarse-mannered, at least set their flocks a better example in the matter of morals than here. The less said about this subject the better; French priests are, whichever way we regard them, objects of commiseration, but there can be no doubt that the indifference shown to religion in the flourishing departement of Seine et Marne has been brought about by the priests themselves and their open disregard of decorum. Their shortcomings in this respect are not hidden, and their domestic lives an open book which all who run may read.

Some of them, however, occupy their time very harmlessly and profitably in gardening and beekeeping, their choicest fruits and vegetables, like those of their neighbours, going to England. We went one day, carrying big baskets with us, to visit the cure of a neighbouring village famous for his green-gages, and certainly the little presbytere looked very inviting with its vine-covered walls and luxuriant flower-gardens. The cure, who told us he had been gardening that morning from four till six o'clock, received us very courteously, yet in a business-like way, and immediately took us to his fruit and vegetable garden some way off. Here we found the greatest possible profusion and evidence of skilful gardening. The fruit-trees were laden, there were Alpine strawberries with their bright red fruit, currants, melons, apricots, &c., and an equal variety of vegetables. Not an inch of ground was wasted, nor were flowers wanting for adornment and the bees--splendid double sun-flowers, veritable little suns of gold, garden mallows, gladiolas and others; a score and more of hives completed the picture which its owner contemplated with natural pride.

"You have only just given your orders in time, ladies," he said; "all my green-gages are to be gathered forthwith for the English market. Ah! those English! those English! they take everything! our best fruit--and the island of Cyprus!"

Whereupon I ventured to rejoin that, at least if we robbed our French neighbours of their best fruit, our money found its way into the grower's pocket. Of course these large purchases in country places make home produce dearer for the inhabitants; but as the English agents pay a higher price than others, the peasants and farmers hail their appearance with delight. The fruit has to ripen on its way, and to enjoy a green-gage, or melon, to the full, we must taste it here. In the autumn the fine pears imported to Covent Garden from these villages sometimes fetch nine sous, four-pence halfpenny each, this being the whole-sale price. No wonder that in retail we have to pay so much.

The cure in question makes a good deal by his bees, and the honey of these parts is first-rate. On the whole, small as is their pay, these parish priests cannot be badly off, seeing that they get extra money by their garden produce, and largely, also, by baptismal and other church fees. Then of course it must be remembered that nothing is expected of them in the way of charity, as is the case with our clergy.

"Nous recevons toujours, nous ne donnons jamais," was the reply of a French bishop on being asked an alms by some benevolent lady for a protege.

Scattered throughout these fertile and prosperous regions are ancient towns, some of which are reached by separate little lines of railway, others are accessible by road only. Coulommiers is one of these, and though there is nothing attractive about it, except a most picturesque old church and a very pretty public walk by the winding river, it is worth making the two hours' drive across country for the sake of the scenery. As there is no direct communication with Couilly, and no possibility of hiring a carriage at this busy season, I gladly accepted a neighbour's offer of a seat in his "trap," a light spring-cart with capital horse. He was a tradesman of the village, and, like the rest of the world here, wore the convenient and cleanly blue cotton trousers and blue blouse of the country. The third spare seat was occupied by a neighbouring notary, the two men discussing metaphysics, literature, and the origin of things, on their way.

We started at seven o'clock in the morning, and lovely indeed looked the wide landscape in the tender light--valley, and winding river, and wooded ridge being soon exchanged for wide open spaces covered with corn and autumn crops. Farming here is carried on extensively, some of these rich farms numbering several hundred acres. The farm-house and buildings, surrounded with a high stone wall, are few and far between, and the separate crops cover much larger tracts than here. It was market-day at Coulommiers, and we passed by many farmers and farmeresses jogging to market, the latter with their fruit and vegetables, eggs and butter, in comfortable covered carts.

Going to market in France means, indeed, what it did with us a hundred years ago; yet the farmers and farmers' wives looked the picture of prosperity. In some cases, fashion had so far got the better of tradition, that the reins were handled by a smart-looking lady in hat and feathers and fashionable dress, but for the most part by toil-embrowned homely women, with a coloured handkerchief twisted round their heads and no pretention to gentility. The men, one and all, wore blue blouses, and were evidently accustomed to hard work, but for all that it was easy to see that they were possessed both of means and intelligence. Like the rest of the Briard population, they are fine fellows, tall, with regular features and frank good-humoured countenances.

Some of these farmers and millers give enormous dowries to their daughters. A million francs is sometimes heard of, and in our own immediate neighbourhood we heard of several rustic heiresses who would have a hundred thousand. Many a farmer, tenant-farmer, too, who toils with his men, has, irrespective of his earnings as a farmer, capital bringing in several thousand francs yearly; in fact, some of them are in receipt of what is considered a fair income for an English curate or vicar, but they work all the same.

At Coulommiers, there is nothing to see but a fine old church with an imposing tower, rising from the centre of the town. I went inside, and, though the doors stood wide open, found it empty, except for a little market-girl, who, having deposited her basket, was bent, not on prayer, but on counting her money. In Brittany, on market-days, there is never a lack of pious worshippers; here it is not so, the good folks of Seine et Marne evidently being inclined to materialism. The interior of this picturesque church is very quaintly coloured, and, as a whole, it is well worth seeing.

Like many other towns in these parts, Coulommiers dates from an ancient period, and long belonged to the English crown. Ravaged during the Hundred Years' War, the religious wars and the troubles of the League, nothing to speak of remains of its old walls and towers of defence. Indeed, except for the drive thither across country, and the fruit and cheese markets, it possesses no temptations for the traveller. Market-day is a sight for a painter. The show of melons alone makes a subject; the weather-beaten market-women, with gay coloured handkerchief twisted round their heads, their blue gowns, the delicious colour and lovely form of the fruit, all this must be seen. Here and there were large pumpkins, cut open to show the ripe red pulp, with abundance of purple plums, apples and pears just ripening, and bright yellow apricots. It was clear les Anglais had not carried off all the fruit! At Coulommiers, as elsewhere, you may search in vain for rags, dirt, or a sign of beggary. Every one is rich, independent, and happy.

CHAPTER III.
PROVINS AND TROYES.

Few travellers in this part of Eastern France turn off the Great Mulhouse line of railway to visit the ancient city of Provins, yet none with a love of the picturesque can afford to pass it by. Airily, nay, coquettishly perched on its smiling, green eminence, and still possessed of an antique stateliness, in striking contrast with the busy little trim town that has sprung up at his feet, Provins captivates the beholder by virtue alike of its uniqueness and poetic charm; I can think of nothing in my various travels at all like this little Acropolis of Brie and Champagne, whether seen in a distance in the railway, or from the ramparts that still encircle it as in the olden time. It is indeed a gem; miniature Athens of a mediaeval princedom, that although on a small scale boasted of great power and splendour; tiny Granada of these Eastern provinces, bearing ample evidence of past literary and artistic glories!

You quit the main line at Longueville, and in a quarter of an hour come upon a vast panorama, crowned by the towers and dome of the still proud, defiant-looking little city of Provins, according to some writers the Agedincum of Caesar's Commentaries, according to others more ancient still. It is mentioned in the capitularies of Charlemagne, and in the Middle Ages was the important and flourishing capital of Basse-Brie and residence of the Counts of Champagne. Under Thibault VI., called Le Chansonnier, Provins reached its apogee of prosperity, numbering at that epoch 80,000 souls. Like most other towns in these parts, it suffered greatly in the Hundred Years' War, being taken by the English in 1432, and retaken from them in the following year. It took part in the League, but submitted to Henry IV. in 1590, and from that time gradually declined; at present it numbers about 7,000 inhabitants only.

The rich red rose, commonly called Provence rose, is in reality the rose of Provins, having been introduced here by the Crusaders from the Holy Land. Gardens of the Provins rose may still be found at Provins, though they are little cultivated now for commercial purpose; Provence, the land of the Troubadours, has therefore no claim whatever upon rose lovers, who are indebted instead to the airy little Acropolis of Champagne. Thus much for the history of the place, which has been chronicled by two gifted citizens of modern time, Opoix and Bourquelot.

It is difficult to give any idea of the citadel, so imposingly commanding the wide valleys and curling rivers at its foot. Leaving the Ville Basse, we climb for a quarter of an hour to find all the remarkable monuments of Provins within a stone's throw--the College, formerly Palace of the Counts of Champagne, the imposing Tour de Cesar, the Basilica of St. Quiriace with its cupola, the famous Grange aux Dimes, the ancient fountain, lastly, the ruined city and gates and walls, called the Ville Haute. All these are close together, but conspicuously towering over the rest are the dome of St. Quiriace, and the picturesque, many pinnacled stronghold vulgarly known as Caesar's Tower. These two crown, not only the ruins, but the entire landscape, for miles around with magnificent effect. The tower itself, in reality having nothing to do with its popular name whatever, but the stronghold of the place built by one of the Counts of Champagne, is a picturesque object, with graceful little pinnacles connected by flying buttresses at each corner, and pointed tower surmounting all, from which now waves proudly the Tricolour flag of the French Republic. A deaf and dumb girl leads visitors through a little flower-garden into the interior, and takes them up the winding stone staircase to see the cells in which Louis d'Outremer and others are said to have been confined. For my own part, I prefer neither to go to the top and bottom of things, neither to climb the Pyramids nor to penetrate into the Mammoth caves of Kentucky. It is much more agreeable, and much less fatiguing, to view everything from the level, and this fine old structure, called Caesar's Tower, is no exception to the rule. Nothing can be more picturesque than its appearance from the broken ground around, above, and below, and no less imposing is the quaint straggling indescribable old church of St. Quiriace close by, now a mere patchwork of different epochs, but in the twelfth and thirteenth centuries one of the most remarkable religious monuments in Brie and Champagne. Here was baptized Thibault VI., the song-maker, the lover of art, the patron of letters, and the importer into Europe of the famous Provence rose; of Thibault's poetic creations an old chronicler wrote:

"C'etait les plus belles chansons, les plus delectables et melodieuses qui oncques fussent ouises en chansons et instruments, et il les fit ecrire en la salle de Provins et en celle de Troyes."

Close to this ancient church is the former palace of Thibault, now a "College Communal," for classic and secondary instruction. Unfortunately the director had gone off for his holiday taking the keys, with him--travellers never being looked for here--so that we could not see the interior and chapel. It is superbly situated, commanding from the terrace a wide view of surrounding country. Perhaps, however, the most curious relics of ancient Provins are the vast and handsome subterranean chambers and passages which are not only found in the Grange aux Dimes literally Tithe-Barn, but also under many private dwellings of ancient date.

Those who love to penetrate into the hovels of the earth may here visit cave after cave, and subterranean chamber after chamber; some of these were of course used for the storage and introduction of supplies in time of war and siege, others may have served as crypts, for purposes of religious ceremony, also a harbour of refuge for priests and monks, lastly as workshops. Provins may therefore be called not only a town but a triple city, consisting, first, of the old; secondly, of the new; lastly, of the underground. Captivating, from an artistic and antiquarian point of view, as are the first and last, all lovers of progress will not fail to give some time to the modern part, not, however, omitting the lovely walls round the ramparts, before quitting the region of romance for plain matter of fact. Here you have unbroken solitude and a wide expanse of open country; you also get a good idea of the commanding position of Provins.

A poetic halo still lingers round the rude times of Troubadour and Knight, but fortunately no such contrast can now be found--at least in France--as there existed between court and people, lord and vassal. The princelings of Brie and Champagne, who lived so jollily and regally in this capital of Provins, knew how to grind down the people to the uttermost, and levied toll-tax upon every imaginable pretext. The Jew had to pay them for his heresy, the assassin for his crime, the peasant for his produce, the artizan for his right to pursue a handicraft.

Now all is good feeling, peace, and prosperity in this modern town, where alike are absent signs of great wealth or great poverty. As yet I am still in a region without a beggar.

Provins affords an excellent example of that spirit of decentralization so usual in France, and unhappily so rare among ourselves. Here in a country town, numbering between seven and eight thousand inhabitants only, we find all the resources of a capital on a small scale; Public Library, Museum, Theatre, learned societies. The Library contains some curious MSS. and valuable books. The Theatre was built by one of the richest and most generous citizens of Provins, M. Gamier, who may be said to have consecrated his ample fortune to the embellishment and advancement of his native town. Space does not permit of an enumeration of the various acts of beneficence by which he has won the lasting gratitude of his fellow-townsmen; and on his death the charming villa he now inhabits, with its gardens, library, art and scientific collections, are to become the property of the town. The Rue Victor Garnier has been appropriately named after this public-spirited gentleman.

There are relics of antiquity to be found in the modern town also; nor have I given anything like a complete account of what is to be found in the old. No one who takes the trouble to diverge from the beaten track in order to visit this interesting little city--Weimar of the Troubadours--will be disappointed. I may add, by the way, that the Hotel de la Boule d'Or, though homely, is comfortable, and that in this out of the way corner the English traveller is invited to partake of the famous "Biere de Bass."

From Provins to Troyes is a three hours' journey by rail; and at Troyes, no matter how impatient the tourist may be to breathe the air of the mountains, he must stop awhile. Here there is so much to see in the way of antiquities that several days might be spent profitably and pleasantly, but for the hotels, of which I have little favourable to say. "Dear and dirty," is the verdict I must pass on the one recommended to me as the best; the fastidious traveller will do well, therefore, so to arrange his journey as to reach Troyes at early morning, and start off again at night; though, of course, such an arrangement will only allow of a hasty glimpse of the various treasures offered to him. Take the churches, for instance. Besides the Cathedral, there are six old churches, each of which has some especial interest, and all deserve to be seen in detail. Then there are picturesque mediaeval houses, one of the first libraries in France, a museum, picture-gallery, &c.

The town itself is cheerful, with decorative bits of window-gardening, hanging dormers, abundance of flowers growing everywhere, and much life animating its old and new quarters. The Cathedral, which rises grandly from the monotonous fields of Champagne, just as Ely towers above the flat plains of our Eastern counties, is also seen to great advantage from the quays, though, when approached nearly, you find it hemmed in with narrow streets. Its noble towers, surmounted by airy pinnacles, and its splendid facade, delight the eye no less than the interior--gem of purest architecture blazing from end to end with rich old stained glass. No light here penetrates through the common medium, and the effect is magical; the superb rose and lancet windows, not dazzling, rather captivating the vision with the hues of the rainbow, being made up, as it seems, with no commoner materials than sapphire, emerald, ruby, topaz, amethyst, all these in the richest imaginable profusion. Other interiors are more magnificent in architectural display, none are lovelier than this, and there is nothing to mar the general harmony, no gilding or artificial flowers, no ecclesiastical trumpery, no meretricious decoration. We find here the glorious art of painting on glass in its perfection, and some of the finest in the Cathedral, as well as in other churches here, are the work of a celebrated Troyen, Linard Gonthier.

A sacristan is always at hand to exhibit the treasury, worth, so it is said, some millions of francs, and which is to be commended to all lovers of jewels and old lace. The latter, richest old guipure, cannot be inspected by an amateur, or, indeed, a woman, without pangs. Such treasures as these, if not appropriated to their proper use, namely dress and decoration, should, at least, be exhibited in the Town Museum, where they might be seen and studied by the artistic. There are dozens of yards of this matchless guipure, but, of course, few eyes are ever rejoiced by the sight of it; and as I turned from one treasure to another, gold and silver ecclesiastical ornaments, carved ivory coffers, enamels, cameos, embroideries, inlaid reliquaries and tapestries, I was reminded of a passage in Victor Hugo's last poem--Le Pape--wherein the Pope of his imagination, thus makes appeal to the Cardinals and Bishops in conclave:

"Pretre, a qui donc as-tu pris tes richesses? Aux pauvres.
Quand l'or s'enfle dans ton sac, Dieu dans ton coeur decroit;
Apprends qu'on est sans pain et sache qu'on a froid.

Les jeunes filles vont rodant le soir dans l'ombre,
Tes rochets, tes chasubles, aux topazes sans nombre,
Ta robe en l'Orient dore s'epanouit,
Sont de spectres qui sont noirs et vivant la nuit.
Que te sert d'empiler sur des planches d'armoires,
Du velours, du damas, du satin, de la moire,
D'avoir des bonnets d'or et d'emplir des tiroirs
Des chapes qu'on dirait couvertes de miroirs?
Oh! pauvres, que j'entends raler, forcats augustes,
Tous ces tresors, chez vous sacres, chez nous sont injustes;
Ce diamant qui met a la mitre un eclair,
Cette emeraude me semble errer toute la mer,
Ces resplendissements sombres de pierreries,
C'est votre sang ...
... Brodes d'or, cousus d'or, chausses d'or, coiffes d'or,
Nous avons des saints Jeans et des saintes Maries,
Que nous emmaillottons dans des verroteries,
Nous depensons Golconde a vetir le neant,
... Pretres, votre richesse est un crime flagrant.
Vos erreurs sont-ils mechants? Non, vos tetes sont dures,
Freres, j'avais aussi sur moi ce tas d'ordures,
Des perles, des onyx, des saphirs, des rubis,
Oui, j'avais sur moi, partout, sur mes habits,
Sur mon ame; mais j'ai vide bien vite
Chez les pauvres."

The sacristan exhibited a tooth of St. Peter and skulls of the saints, but these are treasures we can look on without envy. This little Museum--as, indeed, the Treasury may be called--exposed at the Paris Exhibition of 1867 one of its richest objects, the reliquary of St. Bernard and St. Malachi, a chef-d'oeuvre of the twelfth century; but as some of the jewels were stolen upon that occasion, nothing this year, very naturally, found its way from Troyes Cathedral to the Trocadero.

Close to the Cathedral are the Town Library, Museum, and Picture Gallery, the two first well worth careful inspection. The famous Library has largely contributed to the historic galleries of the Trocadero; but, nevertheless, many exquisite specimens of binding, printing, and illuminating remain; whilst the windows are adorned with most curious and beautiful old glass paintings from the hand of the gifted Linard Gonthier before mentioned. It is hardly necessary to say that strangers are admitted to all the privileges of the reading-room without any form whatever. The library contains a hundred and some odd thousand volumes, besides between two and three thousand rare MSS.

The present population of Troyes is forty thousand; and I am not aware of any small town in England so well off in the matter of books. The Museum is divided into several sections, and, though of recent date, it possesses some interesting and valuable collections. Near the Library and Museum is the most beautiful old church in Troyes, St. Urbain, but as it is unfortunately in the hands of the restorer, we can see nothing of the interior, and the splendid Gothic facade is partly hidden by scaffolding. The traveller may next proceed on a voyage of discovery, coming upon the picturesque Hotel de Ville; quaint relics of mediaeval architecture, and half a dozen old churches, all noteworthy from some point of view.

It is impossible to do more than suggest the rewards that await such an explorer. Troyes, like Angers and Poitiers, abounds in architectural treasures and historical souvenirs; and all these cities cannot be visited too soon. Restoration and renovation are here, as elsewhere, the order of the day, and every year takes something from their character and charm. Two objects, particularly striking amongst so many, shall be mentioned only, as no mere description can convey any idea of the whole. The first is the entrance hall of the Hotel Vauluisant, the features of which should be photographed for the benefit of art-schools and art-decorators generally. The first is a magnificent oak ceiling; the second, a Renaissance chimney piece in carved wood, no less magnificent. The solidity, richness of design, and workmanship of both ceiling and mantel-piece afford an invaluable lesson to artists, whilst beholders can but examine them without a feeling of sadness.

How little we have in modern art-furniture and decoration to be compared with such an achievement: Here we find that cost, labour, and display went for nothing, and artistic perfection alone was aimed at. Not far from the Hotel Vauluisant is Ste. Madeleine, the most ancient church in Troyes, originally Gothic, but now, what with dilapidations and restorations, a curious medley of all various styles. To its architecture, however, the traveller will pay little heed, his whole attention being at once transferred to the famous jube, or rood-loft, or what passes by that name. Bather let me call it a curtain of rare lace cut out in marble, a screen of transparent ivory, a light stalactite roof of some fairy grotto!

On entering, you see nothing but this airy piece of work, one of the daintiest, richest creations of the period, the achievement of Juan Gualde in the sixteenth century. The proportions of the interior seem to diminish, and we cannot help fancying that the church was built for the rood-loft, rather than the rood-loft for the church, so dwarfed is the latter by comparison. The centre aisle is indeed bridged over by a piece of stone-carving, so exquisite in design, so graceful in detail, so airy and fanciful in conception, that we are with difficulty brought to realize its size and solidity. This unique rood-loft measures over six yards in depth, is proportionately long, and is symmetrical in every part, yet it looks as if a breath were only needed to disperse its delicate galleries, hanging arcades, and miniature vaults, gorgeous painted windows forming the background--jewels flashing through a veil of guipure. English travellers may be reminded that Shakespeare's favourite hero, Henry V., was married to Katherine of France in the ancient church of St. Jean at Troyes, now the oldest congeries of different kinds of architecture. The betrothal took place before the high altar of Troyes Cathedral. Lovers of old stained glass must visit St. Nizier and other old churches here; all possess some peculiar interest either within or without.

Troyes--from the standard weight of which we have our Troy weight--is the birth-place of many illustrious men. Mignard the painter, Girardon, sculptor, whose monument to Richelieu in the church of the Sorbonne will not fail to be visited by English travellers, and of the famous painter on glass, Linard Gonthier, who had engraved on his tomb that he awaited the Last Day,

"Sans peur d'etre ecrase."

Among minor accomplishments of the Troyen of to-day, it may be mentioned that nowhere throughout all France--land par excellence of good washing and clear-starching--is linen got up to such perfection as at Troyes. The Blanchisserie

Troyenne is unhappily an art unknown in England. It is curious that, much as cleanliness is thought of among ourselves, we are content to wear linen washed and ironed so execrably as we do. Clean linen in England means one thing, in France another; and no French maid or waiter would put on the half-washed, half-ironed linen we aristocratic insulars wear so complacently. Here indeed is a field for female enterprize!

From Troyes to Belfort is a journey best made by night-mail express, as there is little to see on the way; nor need Belfort--famous for its heroic defence under Danfert, and its rescue from Prussian grasp by the no less heroic pleadings of Thiers--detain the traveller. It is pleasant to find here, as at Troyes, a Rue Thiers, and to see Thiers' portrait in every window. If there is one memory universally adored and respected throughout France, it is that of the "petit bourgeois." No one who gets a glimpse of Belfort with its double ramparts and commanding position, will wonder at Thiers' pertinacity on the one hand, and Bismarck's reluctance on the other. Fortunately the "petit bourgeois" gained his point, and the preservation of Belfort to France was the one drop of comfort in that sea of misery.

CHAPTER IV.
AMONG FRENCH PROTESTANTS
AT MONTBELIARD

Half-an-hour's railway journey brings me to the quaint little town of Montbeliard in the Department of Le Doubs, whose friends' friends give me hearty welcome, and I feel in an hour as much at home as if I had known it all my life. My friends had procured me a little lodging, rather, I should say, a magnificent appartement, consisting of spacious sitting and bedroom, for which I pay one franc a-day. It must not be supposed that Montbeliard is wanting in elegancies, or that the march of refinement is not found here. The fact is, the character of the people is essentially amiable, accommodating, and disinterested, and it never enters into their heads to ask more for their wares, simply because they could get it, or to make capital out of strangers. A franc a day is what is paid in these parts by lodgers, chiefly officers, and no more would be asked of the wealthiest or unwariest. You find the same spirit animating all classes, tradesmen, hotel-keepers, and others, and doubtless this is to be traced to several causes. In the first place, Montbeliard is one of the most enlightened, best educated, and most Protestant departements of all France. Le Doubs, part of the ancient Franche-Comte, is so Protestant, indeed, that in some towns and villages the Catholics are considerably in the minority, as is even the case still at Montbeliard.

So late as the French Revolution, the Comte of this name belonged to Wuertemberg, having passed over to that house by marriage in the fourteenth century. In 1792, however, it became amalgamated with the French Kingdom, and fortunately escaped annexation in the last Franco-German War. Protestantism early took root here, the Anabaptist Doctrine especially, and in the present day Montbeliard numbers several Protestant and only one Catholic church; the former belonging severally to the Reformed Church, the Lutheran, Anabaptists, also two or three so-called Oratoires, or Chapels of Ease, built and supported by private individuals. We find here the tables strangely turned, and in France the unique spectacle of four Protestant pastors to one Catholic priest! At one time the Protestant body numbered two-thirds of the entire population, now the proportion is somewhat less. This still strong Protestant leaven, and the long infiltration of German manners and customs has doubtless greatly modified the character of the inhabitants, who, whether belonging to the one denomination or the other, live side by side harmoniously.

We find a toleration here absolutely unknown in most parts of France, and a generally diffused enlightenment equally wanting where Catholicism dominates. Brittany and Franche-Comté (including the Departments of Le Doubs, Haute Saone, and Jura), offer a striking contrast; in the first we find the priest absolute, and consequently superstition, ignorance, dirt, and prejudice the prevailing order of the day; in the last we have a Protestant spirit of inquiry and rationalistic progress, consequently instruction making vast strides on every side, freedom from bigotry, and freedom alike from degrading spiritual bondage and fanaticism.

In the highly instructive map published by the French Minister of Instruction, Franche-Comté is marked white and Brittany black, thus denoting the antipodes of intellectual enlightenment and darkness to be found in the two countries. Here, indeed, we find ourselves in a wholly different world, so utterly has a spirit of inquiry revolutionized Eastern France, so long has her Western province been held in the grip of the priest. Furthermore, we have evidence of the zeal animating all classes with respect to education on every side, whilst it is quite delightful to converse with a Montbeliardais, no matter to which sect he belongs, so unprejudiced, instructed, and liberal-minded are these citizens of a town neither particularly important, flourishing, nor fortunate. For nine months Montbeliard had to support the presence of the enemy, and though the Prussian soldiery behaved very well here, the amiable, lively little town was almost ruined.

It is no less patriotic than enlightened; republican ideas being as firmly implanted here as any where in France. You see portraits of M. Thiers and Gambetta everywhere, and only good Republican journals on the booksellers' stalls. It would be interesting to know how many copies of the half-penny issue of *La Republique*

Francaise are sold here daily; and whereas in certain parts of France the women read nothing except the Semaine Religieuse and the Petit Journal, here they read the high-class newspapers, reviews, and are conversant with what is going on in the political and literary world at home and abroad. Indeed, the contrast is amazing between female education, so called, in ultra-Catholic and ultra-Protestant France. In Brittany, where the young ladies are educated by the nuns, you never see or hear of a book. The very name of literature is a dead letter, and the upper classes are no better instructed than the lower. In Franche-Comte, girls of all ranks are well educated, young ladies of fortune going in for their brevet, or certificate, as well as those who have their bread to win. They are often familiar with the German and English languages, and above all are thoroughly conversant with their own literature, as well as book-keeping, arithmetic, French history, elementary science, &c.

This little town of eight thousand inhabitants possesses an intellectual atmosphere in which it is possible to breathe. Wherever you go you find books in plenty and of the best kind, and this difference is especially noteworthy among women. I find the young ladies of Montbeliard as familiar with the works of Currer Bell and Mrs. Gaskell as among ourselves. Miss Yonge is also a favourite, and unlike a large class of novel-readers in England, standard works are not neglected by them for fiction. No matter at what time you enter the public library here, you are sure to find ladies of all ages coming to change their books, the contents of this library, be it remembered, consisting chiefly of French classics. The mingled homeliness, diffusion of intelligence and aesthetic culture seen here, remind me of certain little German cities and towns. People living on very modest means find money for books, whereas in certain parts of France no such expenditure is ever thought of, whilst dress and outward show are much less considered.

Naturally, this diffusion of culture raises the tone of conversation and society generally, and its influence is seen in various ways. Music is cultivated assiduously, not only by women of the better ranks, but by both sexes of all, especially among the work-people. The Musical Society of Montbeliard consists of a very respectable orchestra indeed, and is composed of amateurs, mostly young men, recruited from the working as well as middle classes. This Society gives open-air concerts on Sunday afternoons, and one evening in the week, to the great delectation of the multitude, who upon these occasions turn out of doors en masse to enjoy the music and the company of their neighbours. The "Societe d'Emulation" is another instance of the stimulus given to scientific, literary, and artistic pursuits by a Protestant spirit of inquiry. This Society was founded in 1852 by a few savants, in order to develope the public taste for science, art, and letters.

It now numbers two hundred and forty-three members, and has been instrumental in founding a museum containing upwards of eighty thousand archaeological specimens, besides botanical, and geological, and other collections. It is particularly rich in this first respect, few provincial museums having such complete illustrations of the pre-historic and also Gallo-Roman periods. The flint, bronze, and iron epochs are here largely represented, some of the large leaf-shaped flint instruments being particularly beautiful specimens. The excavations at Mandeure--a short drive from Montbeliard--the Epomanduoduum of the Romans--have afforded a precious collection of interesting objects, pottery, small bronze groups of figures, ornaments, terra-cottas, &c.; at Mandeure are to be seen the ruins of the ancient city, amphitheatre, baths, tombs, the vestiges of a temple, and other remains; but excavations are still going on under the direction of the learned President of the "Societe d'Emulation," M. Fabre, and further treasure-trove is looked for.

This charming little museum, so tastefully arranged in the old Halles, by M. Fabre, is open on Sunday afternoon on payment of two sous, but in order to promote a love of science among the young, schools are admitted gratuitously, and within the last ten weeks of summer thirty-nine teachers, and seven hundred and forty-eight pupils of both sexes, had availed themselves of the privilege. During the Prussian occupation in 1870-71, a sum of 323,950 francs was exacted from the town, and the museum and library, after being valued at a considerable sum, were seized as pledges of payment. Seals were set on the collections, and Prussian soldiery guarded the treasures which had been collected with so much zeal and sacrifice. The sum was not paid, but the library and museum were not forfeited, to the satisfaction of all.

There is a charming little Theatre also at the back of the Hotel-de-Ville, where occasional representations by good Parisian companies are given. The decorations are by the hand of one of the artists who decorated the Grand Opera in Paris. He happened to be at Montbeliard, and, taking a kindly interest in the town, offered to do it for a nominal price. Years passed and the promise was forgotten, but, on being reminded of it, the artist, with true French chivalry, redeemed his word, and the decorations of the Montbeliard Theatre are really a magnificent monument of artistic liberality. Montbeliard is as sociable as it is advanced, and one introductory letter from a native of the friendly little town, long since settled in Paris, opened all hearts to me. Everyone is helpful, agreeable, and charming. My evenings are always spent at one pleasant house or another, where music, tea, and conversation lend wings to the cheerful hours. The custom of keeping the veillee, familiar to readers of the gifted Franc-Comtois writer, Charles Nodier, is common here among all classes, people quitting their homes after their early supper--for, according to German habit, we dine at noon and sup at seven here--to enjoy the society of their neighbours.

Delightful recollections did I carry away of many a veillee, and of one in particular, where a dozen friends and their English guest assembled in the summer-house of a suburban garden, there to discuss art, music, literature, and politics, over ices and other good things despatched from the town. We had looked forward to a superb moonlight night with poetic effects of river, chateau, and bridges flooded in silvery light--we had torrents of rain instead, being threatened with what is a phenomenon of no rare occurrence here, namely, an inundation. Situated on the confluence of two rivers, the Allaine and the Lusine, Montbeliard is a quaint, and homely little Venice in miniature, sure to be flooded once or twice a year, when people have to pay visits and carry on their daily avocation in miniature gondolas.

It takes, however, more than minor misfortunes such as these to damp French geniality and good nature, and when our soiree came to an end, everyone returned home well fortified with umbrellas, cloaks, and goloshes in the best possible humour. Sometimes these veillees will be devoted to declamation and story-telling, one or two of the party reading aloud a play or poem, or reciting for the benefit of the rest. In the bitter winter nights this sociable custom is not laid aside, even ladies with their lanterns braving the snow in order to enjoy a little society. Music is the chief out-of-door recreation during the summer months, the military band of the garrison largely contributing to the general amusement.

It is astonishing how French good-humour and light-heartedness help to lighten the hardest lot! We find the hours of toil enormously long here, and economies practised among the better classes of which few English people have any conception. Yet life is made the best of, and everything in the shape of a distraction is seized upon with avidity. Although eminently a Protestant town, shops are open all day long on Sundays, when more business seems to be done than at any other time. The shutters are no sooner put up, however, than everyone goes out for a walk or a visit, and gets as much enjoyment as he can.

Only the rich and exceeding well-to-do people keep servants, others content themselves with a charwoman who comes in for two hours a day, and is paid ten or twelve francs a month, many ladies, by birth and education, living on small means, doing all the lighter household work, marketing, &c., themselves, whilst the small shopkeeping class, who with us must invariably have a wretched drudge, called a maid-of-all-work, never dream of getting anyone to cook or clean for them. As a matter of course, all this is done by the family, no matter how well educated may be its members. We must always bear in mind that the general well-being and easy circumstances of the French middle classes is greatly owing to their freedom from shams. Toil is not regarded as a degradation, and the hateful word "gentility" is not found in their vocabulary. Thus it comes about that you find a mixture of homeliness, comfort, and solidity of fortune, rarely the case in England. Take my landlady as an example, a charming person, who keeps a straw-hat and umbrella shop, whose sister is a repasseuse, or clear-starcher, and whose married brother has also a hat-shop next door. These people do all the work that is to be done themselves, yet in similar circumstances in England would be sure to have maids-of-all-work, nursery-maids, and the rest of it. They have plenty of good furniture, supplies of household and personal linen that would set up a shop, and the children of the brother receive the best possible education he can obtain for them. The elder girl has just returned from Belfort with her first diploma, and is to be sent to Germany to learn German. She has, nevertheless, acquired a knowledge of what all women should know, can cook, clean, cut out and make clothes, &c., and, when she becomes herself a wife and mother, will doubtless exercise all these accomplishments in order to give her children as good an education as she possesses herself. All the family have laid by ample savings.

More might be said about the easy intercourse and geniality of this little town, did space permit. I will pass on to add that though extremely picturesque, with its flower-gardens running down to the water's edge, tiny bridges, hanging roofs, curling rivers, and lastly circling green hills and superb old chateau crowning all, there is little here to detain the tourist. The case is very different with those travellers who are bent upon studying French life under its various aspects, for they will find at Montbeliard a wholly new phase. Much in domestic life reminds us of South Germany, yet no place is more eminently French. The type of physiognomy is frank and animated, fair, and even red hair is common, whilst the stature is above the average, and the general physique gives an idea of strength, character, and health. The Montbeliardins are courteous, but proud and prone rather to bestow than accept favours. Amiability and real goodness of heart especially characterize them.

As a seat of some special manufactures, musical-boxes and clocks being among the chief, it possesses importance; there are also cotton mills, tanneries, foundries, &c. The fabrication of clocks by machinery is a curious process, the precision and apparent intelligence of the machines being as agreeable to contemplate as the reverse is humiliating: namely, the spectacle of men, women, and children being converted into automatons by unremitting mechanical labour. The length of the day's work here is prodigious, consisting of twelve sometimes fourteen hours, and the occupation extremely unwholesome, owing to the smell of the oil and the perpetual noise of machinery. The pay is low, beginning at three francs and reaching to four or four and a half a day. We may blame the artizan class for improvidence, insobriety, and many other failings, but none who calmly compare the life of a clock-maker, for instance, condemned to spend twelve hours of the twenty-four in this laborious, unwholesome, and ill-remunerated labour, with that of the better classes, can wonder at his discontent. If he seeks to better his position by means of strikes, socialistic schemes, or other violent means, at least we must grant that it is only natural, till some other should offer themselves.

It is to be hoped that the hours of labour will soon be shortened in a part of France so advanced in other respects, and meantime artizans here are better off than elsewhere. All round the town you find so-called cites ouvrieres, built on the model of those of Mulhouse; little streets of cheerful cottages, each with its bit of flower and vegetable-garden, where at least the workman has something to call a home after his day's labour. These artizan quarters are well or ill-kept, of course, according to the thrift or slovenliness of the tenants; some are charming, but at their worst they are a vast improvement upon the close, ill-ventilated quarters to be found in towns. They are also much cheaper, about L5 a year being charged for both house and garden, whereas, even in a little town like Montbeliard, accommodation is dear and difficult to be had. In fact, without these villages the question of house-room would be as much of a problem here for the workman as among our own rural population; no doubt the heads of firms who have built cheerful and ornamental little rows of English-like cottages for their workpeople were actuated at the same time chiefly by philanthropic motives, but they found it absolutely necessary to take some steps in the matter.

Various efforts are being made to raise the status of the mechanic by means of lectures, reading-rooms, and recreation, but, whilst the hours of labour remain what we find them, little good can be effected. A devoted lady, who has spent her whole life in her native town, has done much for the female part of the manufacturing population by means of free night-schools, free library, chiefly for the young, Sunday afternoon classes for the teaching of cutting-out and needle-work, and recreation combined, gratuitous laundries, and other philanthropic schemes. These efforts of Mademoiselle Rosalie Morel, a lay-woman, have been seconded by those of a Protestant deaconess in another direction, the latter devoting herself to nursing and the teaching of hygiene and sanitary science. In the matter of cleanliness, therefore, these good people are not left in the dark as in benighted Brittany, where dirt is not preached against as it ought to be in the pulpit. Mademoiselle Morel's free laundries, in other words a scheme set on foot for the purpose of teaching the poorest classes what clean linen should be, have doubtless effected much good, and on the whole cleanliness is the rule here, and the public hot and cold baths much frequented by all.

In spite, however, of the animation and bonhomie of this little town, there is a dark side to social life, and in the train of intemperance and unthrift among the manufacturing population, we find squalor and immorality. After several weeks' sojourn in that Utopia of all socialistic dreamers--a land without a beggar!--I found myself here, once more, in the domains of mendicity, though it is not to be found to any great extent. The custom of putting out infants to nurse is, fortunately, unfrequent in these parts, and, as a natural consequence, infant mortality is not above the average. The cites ouvrieres are to be thanked for this, and the nearness of the home to the factory enables the baby to be brought to its mother for nourishment, and in our visit to the clock manufactory before spoken of, we saw mothers nursing their infants on the spot. Nearer Paris, you constantly encounter infants three day's old being dispatched with their foster-mother into some country place, there to be brought up by hand, in other words, to die; but here it is not so. We find on a small scale at Montbeliard that contrast between wealth and poverty seen in England, but wholly absent from the rural districts of France. The aristocracy of the place here is composed of the wealthy manufacturing class, and by little and little Parisian luxuries are finding their way into this remote region. Until within quite recent date, for instance, there was no such thing as a stand for hackney carriages here; now it has become the fashion to take drives in fine weather. In our walks and drives in the neighbourhood, we encounter handsome waggonettes and open carriages with a pair of horses, rarely seen in the purely agricultural districts.

In every way, habits of life have become modified by the rapid rise of a commercial aristocracy; and, as a natural consequence, we find much more social distinction than in those parts of France where no such class exists. Yet a stranger, who should study French manners and customs for the first time, would find the principle of equality existing in a degree unknown in England. Can anything be more absurd than the differences of rank that divide the population of our provincial towns? The same thing is seen in the country, where the clergyman holds aloof from the village doctor, the farmer from the shopkeeper, both these from the village schoolmaster, and where, indeed, everybody thinks himself better than his neighbour.

We have, in English provincial towns, schools for the professional classes, schools for the children of farmers, of wholesale shopkeepers, of small retail tradesmen; lastly, schools for the "people," and you no more expect to find a rich man's child attending the latter than a chimney-sweep's son at the Grammar School. In French country towns all this is simplified by the Ecole Communale, at which boys and girls respectively, no matter what their parents' calling or means, receive precisely the same education; after the Ecole Communale, comes the College, where a liberal education is afforded to boys, and pupils study for the examination of Bachelier-es-Lettres et Sciences, but are not prepared as at the Lycees for the "Doctorate-in-Law." There is no other school here for primary instruction of both sexes but the Communal School, Protestant and Catholic, whither all the children, rich and poor, patrician and proletaire, go as a matter of course. The politeness of the French working-classes may be partly accounted for in the association of all ranks in early life. Convent, or other schools, for young ladies, do not exist at Montbeliard, and those who study for the first and second diploma are generally prepared at Belfort and Besancon, where the examinations are held.

There is also here an Ecole Normale, training school for teachers; also a Protestant training school, noted for its excellence. On the whole, for a town of eight thousand inhabitants, Montbeliard must be considered rich in educational and intellectual resources.

Much of the farming in these parts is tenant-farming on a fair scale, i.e., fifty to two or three hundred acres. In the case of small peasant properties, which, of course, exist also, the land is usually not divided on the death of the father, the eldest son purchasing the shares of his brothers and sisters. More on the subject of agriculture will be said further on, there being nothing particularly striking about the two tenant-farms I visited with friends in the immediate proximity of the town. The first, though not a model farm, is considered a good specimen of farming on a large scale, the size being two hundred and fifty acres, hired at a rental of fifty francs per hectare, or about a pound per acre. The premises are large and handsome, and cleanly, according to a French agricultural standard, and, as usual, with a large heap of manure drying up in the sun. Here we found thirty-five splendid Normandy and other cows, entirely kept for milking, the milk being all sent to Montbeliard, with a small number of bullocks, horses and pigs. The land looks poor, and gives no evidence of scientific farming, though very few improvements are made, new agricultural methods and implements introduced, and thus the resources of the land developed. The farmer's wife and daughters were all hard at work, and the farmer busy with his men in the fields. Close to the farm-house, which we found spacious and comfortable, is the handsome villa of the owner, who has thus an opportunity of seeing for himself how things go. If tenant-farming does not pay in England, it certainly can only do so in France by means of a laboriousness and economy of which we have hardly an idea. Work, indeed, means one thing with us, and quite another with our French neighbour.

It is on market-day that the country folks and their wares are to be seen to the best advantage; and housekeepers supply themselves with butter, fruit, vegetables and haberdashery, all being very cheap; peaches sixpence a pound, melons two or three sous each, and so on in proportion. One fruit may puzzle strangers, it is the red berry of the cultivated service berry tree, and makes excellent preserve. In spite, however, of the low prices of garden and orchard produce, everyone complains that the cost of living has greatly risen even here since the war, and that many provisions are as dear as in Paris. Yet, as far as I can judge, Montbeliard is still a place in which, if you cannot live on nothing a year, you can live on next to nothing, and not uncomfortably either.

And now, before turning "to fresh fields and pastures new," a word must be said about the illustrious name that will ever be linked with Montbeliard. Many a hasty traveller alights at the railway station for the purpose of seeing the noble monument of David d'Angers, and the antiquated humble dwelling bearing the proud inscription:

"Ici naquit George Cuvier."

The bronze statue of the great anatomist stands out in bold relief before the Hotel-de-Ville, the profile being turned towards the house in which he first saw the light, the full face fronting the large Protestant Church built in 1602, a century and a half before his birth. The proximity is a happy one, for was it not by virtue of Protestantism, no matter how imperfectly manifested, that Cuvier was enabled to pursue his inquiries with such magnificent results? Two centuries before, he might, like Galileo, have had to choose between martyrdom or scientific apostasy. The great Montbeliardais--whose brain weighed more than that of any human being ever known--is represented with a pen in one hand, a scroll in the other, on which is drawn the anatomy of the human frame. He wears the long, full frock coat of the period, its ample folds having the effect of drapery. David d'Angers has achieved no nobler work than this statue.

The College of Montbeliard, called after its greatest citizen, was founded a few years ago, and is one of the first objects seen on quitting the railway station of the Rue Cuvier.

English tourists do not often turn aside from the Swiss route to visit the quieter beauties of the Department of the Doubs, and residents here regret the absence of travellers, which, of course, tells upon the hotels. No one has a word to say in favour of anything we are likely to meet with on our journey throughout the length or breadth of Franche Comte. When it is as much of a recreation ground with us as Switzerland, doubtless everything will change, but nothing daunted we pursue our journey. The only way to see this country to perfection is to hire a carriage for the day, and retain it as long as you please. The railway does not penetrate into the most picturesque regions, and the diligence is slow and inconvenient. Accordingly, having had an itinerary written out for us by friends who had gone over every inch of the ground, mostly on foot, I set off with an enterprising lady, a native of these parts, for a few days' drive in the most romantic scenery of the Doubs, southward of Montbeliard, and in the direction of Switzerland. So well is the road marked out for us that we want neither "Joanne" nor "Murray," and we have, moreover, procured the services of a coachman who has been familiarized with the country by thirty years' experience. Thus far, therefore, we have nothing to desire but fine weather, which has been very rare since my arrival; tempests, showers, and downpours being the order of the day. However, choosing one morning of unusual promise, we start off at seven o'clock, prepared for the best or the worst; a description of the superb pine-forests and romantic valleys of the Doubs being reserved for the next chapter.

CHAPTER V.
ST. HIPPOLYTE, MORTEAU, AND THE SWISS BORDERLAND.

I never understood, till I travelled with French friends, why hotels in France should be so bad, but the reason is to be sought in that amiability, laisser faire, call it by what name we will, that characteristic which distinguishes our neighbours on the other side of La Manche. We English, who perpetually travel, growl and grumble at discomfort till, by force of persistent fault-finding, we bring about reformation in hotels and travelling conveniences generally--whereas the French, partly from a dislike of making themselves disagreeable, partly from the feeling that they are not likely to go over the same ground again, leave things as they find them, to the great disadvantage of those who follow. The French, indeed, travel so little for mere pleasure that, whenever they do so, they think it useless to make a fuss about what seems to them a part and parcel of the journey. Thus it happens that, wherever you go off the beaten tracks in France, you find the hotels as bad as they can well be, and your French fellow-traveller takes the dirt, noise, and discomfort generally much as a matter of course. I am sorry that I can say little for the hotels we found throughout our four days' drive in the most romantic scenery of the Doubs, for the people are so amiable, obliging, and more titan moderate in their charges, that one feels inclined to forgive anything. Truth must be told, however, and so, for once, I will only add that the tourist must here be prepared for the worst in the matter of accommodation, whilst too much praise cannot be accorded to the general desire to please, and absolute incapacity of these good people to impose on the stranger.

It must also be explained that as the mere tourist is a rare phenomenon in these remote parts, the hotels are not arranged in order to meet his wants, but those of the commis-voyageur, or commercial traveller, who is the chief and best customer of innkeepers all over the country. You meet no one else at the table-d'hote but the commis-voyageurs, and it must not be supposed that they are in any way objectionable company. They quietly sit out the various courses, then retire to the billiard-room, and they are particularly polite to ladies. Throughout the journey we were on the borders of Switzerland, the thinnest possible partition dividing the land of cleanliness, order, and first-rate accommodation from that of dirt, noise, and discomfort; yet so rigid is the demarcation that no sooner do you put foot on Swiss ground than you find the difference. Quite naturally, English travellers keep on the other side of the border, and only a stray one now and then crosses it.

Our little caleche and horse left much to desire, but the good qualities of our driver made up for everything. He was a fine old man, with a face worthy of a Roman Emperor, and, having driven all over the country for thirty years, knew it well, and found friends everywhere. Although wearing a blue cotton blouse, he was in the best sense of the word a gentleman, and we were somewhat astonished to find him seated opposite to us at our first table-d'hote breakfast. We soon saw that he well deserved the respect shown him; quiet, polite, dignified, he was the last person in the world to abuse his privileges, never dreaming of familiarity. The extreme politeness shown towards the working classes here by all in a superior social station doubtless accounts for the good manners we find among them. My fellow-traveller, the widow of a French officer, never dreamed of accosting our good Eugene without the preliminary Monsieur, and did not feel herself at all aggrieved at having him for her vis-a-vis at meals. Eugene, like the greater part of his fellow-countrymen, is proud and economical, and, in order not to become dependent upon his children, or charity, in his old age, had already with his savings bought a house and garden. It is impossible to give any idea of the thrift and laboriousness of the better order of working classes here.

Soon after quitting Montbeliard we began to ascend, and for the rest of the day were climbing, gradually exchanging the region of corn-fields and vineyards for that of the pine. From Montbeliard to St. Hippolyte is a superb drive of about five hours, amid wild gorges, grandiose rocks that have here taken every imaginable form--rampart, citadel, fortress, tower, all trellised and tasselled with the brightest green; and narrow mountains, valleys, here called "combes"--delicious little emerald islands shut in by towering heights on every side. The mingled wildness and beauty of the scenery reach their culminating point at St. Hippolyte, a pretty little town with picturesque church, superbly situated at the foot of three mountain gorges and the confluence of the Doubs with the Dessoubre, the latter river here turning off in the direction of Fuans. Here we halt for breakfast, and in two hours' time are again ascending, looking down from a tremendous height at the town, incomparably situated in the very heart of these solitary passes and ravines. Our road is a wonderful bit of achievement, curling as it does around what below appear unapproachable precipices, and from the beginning of our journey to the end, we never ceased admiring it. This famous road was constructed with many others in Louis Philippe's time, and must have done great things for the progress of the country. Excepting an isolated little chateau here and there, and an occasional diligence and band of cantonniers, all is solitary, and the solitariness and grandeur increase as we leave the region of rocks and ravines to enter that of the pine--still getting higher and higher. From St. Hippolyte to our next halting place, Maiche, the road only quits one pine-forest to enter another, our way now being perfectly solitary, no herdsman's hut in sight, no sound of bird or animal, nothing to break the silence. Some of these trees are of great height--their sombre foliage at this season of the year being relieved by an abundance of light brown cones, which give them the appearance of gigantic Christmas trees hung with golden gifts. Glorious as is the scenery we had lately passed, hoary rocks clothed with richest green, verdant slopes, valleys, and mountain sides all glowing in the sunshine--the majestic gloom and isolation of the pine-forests appeal more to the imagination, and fill the mind with deeper delight. Next to the sea, the pine-forest, to my thinking, is the sublimest of nature's handiworks. Nothing can lessen, nothing can enlarge such grandeur as we have here. Sea and pine-forest are the same, alike in thunder-cloud or under a serene sky--summer and winter, lightning and rain--we can hardly add by a hairbreadth to the profundity of the impression they produce.

Maiche might conveniently be made a summer resort, and I can fancy nothing healthier and pleasanter than such a sojourn around these fragrant pines. The hotel, too, from what we saw of it, pleased us greatly, and the landlady, like most of the people we have to do with in these parts, was all kindness, obligingness, and good-nature. In large cities and cosmopolitan hotels, a traveller is Number one, two, or three, as the case may be and nothing more. Here, host and hostess interest themselves in all their visitors, and regard them as human beings. The charges moreover are so trifling that, in undertaking a journey of this kind, hotel expenses need hardly count at all--the real cost is the carriage.

From Maiche to Le Russey, our halting place for the night, is a distance of three hours only, during which we are still in the pine-woods. Le Russey possesses no attractions, except a quaint and highly artistic monument to the memory of one of her children, a certain Jesuit missionary, whose imposing statue, cross in hand, is conspicuously placed above the public fountain. We cannot have too many of these local monuments, unfortunately rarer in England than in France. They lend character to provincial towns, and keep up a spirit of patriotism and emulation among the people. The little town of Le Russey should, if possible, be halted at for an hour or two only, the hotels are dirty and uncomfortable; we fared worse there than I ever remember to have fared in France--which is saying a good deal!

Next morning we were off at eight o'clock; our road, now level for the most part, leading us through very different scenery from that of the day before, monotonous open country, mostly pasturage, with lines of pine and fir against the horizon--in many places were rocky wastes, hardly affording scant herbage for the cattle. Much of this scenery reminded me of the Fell district or North Wales, but by degrees we entered upon a far more interesting region. We were now close to Switzerland, and the landscape already wore a Swiss look. There is nothing prettier in a quiet way than this Swiss borderland, reached after a long stretch of dreary country; here we have grace without severity, beauty without gloom, pastoral hills and dales alive with the tinkling of cattle-bells, and pleasingly diversified with villages scattered here and there; a church spire rising above the broad-roofed, white-washed chalets on every side, undulating green pastures, in some places shut in by pine-clad ridges, in others by smiling green hills. We see patches of corn still too green to cut, also bits of beet-root, maize, hemp, and potatoes; the chief produce of these parts is of course that of the dairy, the "Beurre de Montagne," being famous in these parts. Throughout our journey we have never lost sight of the service-berry tree; the road from Maiche to Morteau is indeed planted with them, and nothing can be handsomer than the clusters of bright red, coral-like berries we have on every side. The hedges show also the crimson-tasselled fruit of the barberry, no less ornamental than the service-berry tree. It is evident the greatest possible care is taken of these wayside plantations, and in a few years' time the road will present the appearance of a boulevard. At La Chenalotte, a hamlet half way between Le Russey and Morteau, enterprising pedestrians, may alight and take a two hours' walk by a mountain path to the Falls of the Doubs; but as the roads were very bad on account of the late heavy rains, we prefer to drive on to the little hamlet of Les Pargots, beyond Morteau, and from thence reach the falls by means of a boat, traversing the lake of Les Brenets and the basin of the Doubs. The little Swiss village of Les Brenets is coquettishly perched on a green hill commanding the lake, and we are now indeed on Swiss ground, being within a few miles only of Chaux de Fonds, and a short railway journey of Neufchatel and Pontarlier.

We trust ourselves to the care of an experienced boatwoman, and are soon in a fairy-like scene, a long sheet of limpid water surrounded by verdant ridges, amid which peep chalets here and there, and velvety pastures slope down to the water's edge; all is here tenderness, loveliness, and peace. As we glide from the lake to the basins, the scenery takes a severer character, and there is sublimity in these gigantic walls of rock rising sheer from the silvery lakelike sheets of water, each successive one seeming to us more beautiful and romantic than the last. Perfect solitude reigns here, for so precipitous and steep are these fortress-like rocks that there is no "coigne of vantage," even for the mountain goat, not the tiniest path from summit to base, no single break in the shelving masses, some of which take the weirdest forms. Seen as we first saw them with a brilliant blue sky overhead, no shadow on the gold green verdure, these exquisite little lakes--twin pearls on a string--afford the daintiest, most delightful spectacle; but a leaden sky and a driving wind turn this scene of enchantment into gloom and monotony, as we find on our way back.

The serene beauty of the lake, and the imposing aspect of these rock-shut basins give an ascending scale of beauty, and the climax is reached when, having glided in and out from the first to the last, we alight, climb a mountain path, and behold far below at our feet, amid a deafening roar, the majestic Falls of the Doubs.

Such things are indescribable; but to come from the sublime to the ludicrous, I would advise future travellers not to follow our example in respect of a woman-boatman. The good woman, who acted as guide to the Falls could not hold her tongue for a single moment, and her loud inharmonious tittle-tattle put us in ill-humour for the rest of the day. When you make a long journey to see such a phenomenon as this, you should see it alone, or, at least, in perfect quiet. We had come opportunely for the Falls, however, the enormous quantity of rain that had fallen within the last few weeks having greatly augmented their volume. It was as if no river, but a sea were leaping from its prison here, rejoiced to leave its rocky home and follow its own wild way. The profound impression created by such a scene as this, to my thinking, lies chiefly in the striking contrast we have here before us--a vast eddy of snow-white foam, the very personification of impetuous movement, also of lightness, sparkling whiteness, with a background of pitchy black rock, still, immoveable, changeless, as the heavens above.

As we stood thus lost, peering down at the silvery whirlpools and its sombre environment, we were bedewed with a light mist, spray sent upward by the frothing waters. Our terrible female Cerberus gabbled on, and so to be rid of her we descended. There is a Restaurant on the French, also on the Swiss side of the basin we had just crossed, and we chose the latter, not with particular success. Very little we got either to eat or drink, and a very long while we had to wait for it, but at last we had dined, and again embarked to cross the basin and lake. In the meantime the weather had entirely changed, and, instead of a glowing blue sky and bright sun, we had hovering clouds and high winds, making our boatwoman's task difficult in the extreme. However she continued to clear one little promontory after another, and, when once out of the closely confined basins on to the more open lake, all was as easy as possible.

We found the Hotel Gimbard at Morteau a vast improvement upon that of Le Russey, and woke up refreshed next morning after having well supped and well slept, to find, alas! thunder, lightning, and torrents of rain the order of the day. The programme had been to turn off at Morteau in the direction of Fuans and the picturesque banks of the Dessoubre, reaching St. Hippolyte at night, but with great reluctance we were now obliged to give up this round. From Morteau to St. Hippolyte is a day's journey, only to be made by starting at eight in the morning, and there are not even decent wayside inns. So we patiently waited till the storm was over, and as by that time it was past midday, there was nothing to do but drive leisurely back to Maiche. More fortunate travellers than ourselves, in the matter of weather, however, are particularly recommended the other route. Maiche is a good specimen of the large, flourishing villages, or bourgs, found in these parts, and a greater contrast with those of Brittany cannot be conceived. There you find no upper or middle-class element, no progress, little communication with the outer world; some of the towns even, St. Pol de Leon, for instance, being literally asleep. Here all is life, bustle, and animation, and, though we are now amid a Catholic community, order and comparative cleanliness prevail. Some of the cottage gardens are quite charming, and handsome modern homes in large numbers denote the existence of rich bourgeois families, as is also the case in the villages near Montbeliard. The commune of Maiche has large revenues, especially in forest lands, and we can thus account for the really magnificent cure, or presbytere, the residence of the cure, also the imposing Hotel-de-Ville, and new costly decoration of the church. There is evidently money for everything, and the cure of Maiche must be a happy person, contrasting his position favorably with that of his fellow-cures in the Protestant villages around Montbeliard. The down-hill drive from our airy eminence amid the pine-forests was even more striking than our ascent two days before; and we naturally got over the ground in less than half the time. It is a pity such delightful scenery as this should not be made more accessible to travellers by a first rate inn. There are several hotels at Maiche, also at St. Hippolyte and Pont de Roide, but they are adapted rather to the wants of the commis-voyageur than the tourist. Yet there is a friendliness, a bonhomie, and disinterestedness about the hotel-keepers, which would soon disappear were Franche Comte turned into a little Switzerland. At the table-d'hote dinner, the master of the house always presides and looks after the guests, waiters there are none; sometimes the plates are changed by the landlady, who also superintends the kitchen, sometimes by the landlord, sometimes by a guest, and shortcomings are always made up for by general geniality. Everyone knows everyone, and the dinner is a meeting of old friends.

All this will soon be changed with the new line of railway to lead from Besancon by way of St. Hippolyte and Morteau into Switzerland, and future travellers will be able to see this beautiful country with very little fatigue. As yet Franche Comte is an unknown region, and the sight of an English tourist is of rare occurrence. When we leave Pont de Roide, we once more enter the region of Protestantism, every village possessing a Protestant as well as a Catholic Church. The drive to

Blamont is charming--a bit of Devonshire, with green lanes, dells, and glades, curling streams and smooth pastures. Blamont itself is romantically situated, crossing a verdant mountain side, its twin spires (Protestant and Catholic) rising conspicuously above the scattered villages; beyond these, the low mountain range of Blamont.

We have been all this time, be it remembered, geographically speaking in the Jura, though departmentally in the Doubs, the succession of rocks and mountains passed through forming part of the Jura range which vanishes in the green slopes of Blamont.

The next village, Glaye, is hardly less picturesque, and indeed all this neighbourhood would afford charming excursions for the pedestrian. The rest of our drive lay through an open, fairly-cultivated plain with little manufacturing colonies, thickly scattered among the rural population. In many cases the tall black chimneys spoil the pastoralness of the scene.

It was with extreme regret I took farewell of the friendly little Protestant town of Montbeliard, soon after this journey. I had entered it a few weeks before, a stranger, I quitted it amid the good wishes, hand-clasps, and affectionate farewells of a dozen kind friends. Two hours' railway journey, through a beautiful country, brought me to Besancon, where, as at Montbeliard, I received the warmest welcome, and felt at home at once.

CHAPTER VI.
BESANCON AND ITS ENVIRONS.

The hotels at Besancon have the reputation of being the worst in all France, but my kind friends would not let me try them. I found myself, therefore, all at once in the midst of all kinds of home comforts, domesticities, and distractions, with delightful cicerones in host and hostess, and charming little companions in their two children. This is the poetry of travel; thus to journey from one place to another, provided with introductory letters which open hearts and doors at every stage, and make each one the inauguration of a new friendship. I wish I could subjoin an illustration of "How I travelled through Franche-Comte," for my exploration of these regions was a succession of pic-nics--host, hostess, their English guest, Swiss nurse-maid, and two little fair-haired boys, being cosily packed in an open carriage; on the seat beside the driver, a huge basket, suggesting creature comforts, the neck of a wine bottle, and the spout of a tea-pot being conspicuous above the other contents. This is indeed the way I saw the beautiful valley of the Doubs, and not only the country round about Besancon, but the border-land of Switzerland and Savoy. The weather--we are in the first days of September--is perfect. The children, aged respectively eighteen months and three years and odd, are the best little travellers in the world, always going to sleep when convenient to their elders, and at other times quietly enjoying the shifting landscape; in fact, there is nothing to mar our enjoyment of regions as lovely as any it has ever been my good fortune to witness.

In consequence of the bad character of the Besancon hotels, even French tourists seldom break their journey here; but, on the opening of the new railway line into Switzerland, joining Besancon, Ornans, and Morteau, new and better hotels are sure to spring up. At present, wherever we go, we never, by any chance, meet the ubiquitous English traveller with his Murray, and my friends here say that, during a several years' residence in Besancon, they have never even yet seen such an apparition! Yet Franche-Comte, at present a terra incognita of tourists, abounds in all kinds of beauty; the sublime, the gracious, the grandiose, and the pastoral, rock, vast panoramas, mountain and valley, all are here; and all as free from the trace of the English and American tourist as the garden of Eden before Eve's trespass!

Besides these quieter beauties are some rare natural phenomena, such as the Glaciere de la Grace Dieu, near Baume-les-Dames, and the famous Osselle grottoes, both of which may be reached by railway. We preferred, however, the open carriages the basket and the tea-pot, and accordingly set off for the latter one superb morning in the highest spirits, which nothing occurred to mar. Quitting this splendid environment of Besancon, we drive for three hours amid the lovely valley of the Doubs, delighted at every bend of the road with some new feature in the landscape; then choosing a sheltered slope, unpacked our basket, lunched al fresco, with the merriest spirits, and the heartiest appetite. Never surely did the renowned Besancon pates taste better, never did the wine of its warm hill-sides prove of a pleasanter flavour! The children sported on the turf like little Loves, the air was sweet with the perfume of new-made hay. The birds sang overhead, and beyond our immediate pavilion of greenery, lay the curling blue river and smiling green hills. Leaving the children to sleep under the trees, and the horse to feed at a neighbouring mill--there is no kind of wayside inn here, so we have to beg a little hay from the miller or a farmer--we follow a little lad, provided with matches and candles to the entrance of the famous grottoes. Outside the sugar-loaf hill, so marvellously channelled and cased with stalactite formation, has nothing remarkable--it is a mere green height, and nothing more. Inside, however, as strange a spectacle meets our eyes as it is possible to conceive. To see these caves in detail, you must spend an hour or two in the bowels of the earth, but we were contented with half that time, for this underground promenade is a very chilly one, as in some places we were ankle deep in water. Each provided with a candle, we now follow our youthful guide, who was accompanied by a dog, as familiar as himself with the windings of these sombre subterranean palaces, for palaces they might be called. Sometimes the stalactite roofs are lofty, sometimes we have to bend our heads in order to pass from one vaulted chamber to another; here we have a superb column supporting an arch; here a pillar in course of formation, everywhere the strangest, most fantastic architecture, an architecture moreover that is the work of ages; one petrifying drop after another doing its apportioned work, column, arch, and roof being formed by a process so slow that the life-time of a human being hardly counts in the calculation. There is something sublime in the contemplation of this steady persistence of Nature, this undeviating march to a goal; and as we gaze upon the embryo stages of the petrifaction, stalagmite patiently lifting itself upward, stalactite as patiently bending down to the remote but inevitable union, we might almost fancy them sentient agents in the marvellous transformation. The stamens of a passion-flower do not more eagerly, as it seems, coil upwards to embrace the pistil; the beautiful stamina flower of the Vallisneria spiralis does not more determinately seek its mate than these crystal pendants covet union with their fellows below. Their perpetual bridals are accomplished after countless cycles of time, whilst meantime in the sunlit world outside, the faces of whole continents are being changed, and entire civilizations are formed and overthrown.

The feeble light projected by our four candles in these gloomy yet majestic chambers was not so feeble as to obscure the insignificant names of hundreds of individuals scrawled here and there. The great German philosopher Schopenhauer is at pains philosophically to explain the foolish propensity of travellers to perpetuate their names, or as it so seems to them. The Pyramids or Kentucky Caves do not impress their minds at all, but to see their own illustrious names John Brown and Tom Smith cut upon them, does seem a very interesting and important fact. The bones of the Cave bear and other gigantic animals have been formed here; but the principal tenants of these antique vaults are now the bats, forming huge black clusters in the roof. There is something eerie in their cries, but they are more alarmed than alarming; the lights disturbing them not a little.

Pleasant after even this short adventure into the regions of the nether-world, was the return to sunshine, green trees, the children, and the tea-pot! After calling it into requisition, we set off homewards, reaching Besancon just as the moon made its appearance, a large silver disc above the purple hills; and the next day, good luck still following us, we had a drive and pic-nic in the opposite direction, this time with a less ambitious programme. In fact, we were merely accepting a neighbour's invitation to a friendly dinner out of doors, a few miles from Besancon. This pic-nic is a fair sample of Franche-Comte hospitality; not only friends were invited but their guests, babies, servants, and "all that was in their house," the various parties being collected by the host in a waggonette. It was Sunday, and though I am here still in a strictly Protestant atmosphere, host and guests being Protestants, it was pleasant to find none of the Puritanism characterizing some sections of the Reformed Church in France. The Protestant pastor, indeed, to whose eloquent discourse I had listened that morning, was of the party; and it is quite a matter of course here to spend Sunday afternoons thus sociably and healthfully. The meeting-place was a rustic spot much resorted to by Bisontins on holidays, and easily reached from the little station of Roche on the railway line to Belfort. A winding path through a wood leads to the so-called Acier Springs, which, since the Roman epoch, have continued to supply Besancon with the delicious water we find here in such abundance. We have just such bits of wood, waterfalls, and mountains in North Wales, but seldom in September such unbroken sunshine to make a pic-nic exactly what it should be. It was warm enough for July, and young and old could disport themselves on the turf in perfect security.

As the afternoon wore on, numerous pleasure-parties, mostly belonging to the working-classes, found their way to the same pleasant spot, all amply provided with baskets of wine and provisions. Some went further in search of a little glade they could have to themselves, others took possession of nooks and corners in the open space where we tad just before dined so merrily. It was amusing to see how little attention these good people paid to us, or any other outsiders. Two or three of the women, fearing to tear their Sunday gowns in the wood, coolly took them off, hung them on the trees near, and as coolly re-made their toilette when their woodland rambles were over.

The train to Roche certainly brought in a goodly contingent of pic-nic parties that afternoon and when about four o'clock we prepared to return home, the place was beginning to wear a very animated appearance. The moon had risen ere we reached our destination, and, seen in the tender summer twilight, the valley of the Doubs looked even more beautiful than in the glowing sunshine of mid-day. There is no monotony in these vine-clad hills, rugged mountain sides wooded from peak to base, close shut valleys, and bright blue winding rivers; whether seen under the dropping shadows of a shifting sky, or under the glow of sunset, their quiet beauties delight the eye of the mere spectator and commend themselves to the artist. Perhaps no Department in France is richer in rivers than Le Doubs, every landscape has its bit of river, rivulet or canal.

To get an idea of the commanding position of Besancon, we must climb one of these lofty green heights, that of Notre Dame des Buis, for instance, an hour's drive from the town. Having reached a sharp eminence, crowned by a chapel and covered with box-wood, we obtain a splendid view of the natural and artificial defences which make Besancon, strategically speaking, one of the strongest positions in France. Caesar, in his 'Commentaries' speaks almost with enthusiasm of the admirable[2] position of Vesontio, the capital of the Sequani, and, when he became master of it, the defeat of Vercingetorix was a mere matter of time. But what would the great general have said, could be have seen his citadel thus dwarfed into insignificance by Vauban's magnificent fortifications? and what would be Vauban's amazement could he behold the stupendous works of modern strategists?

Beyond these proudly-cresting heights, every peak bristling with its defiant fort, stretches a vast panorama; the mountain chains of the Jura, the Vosges, the snow-capped Swiss Alps, the plains of Burgundy, all these lie under our eye, clearly defined in the transparent atmosphere of this summer afternoon. The campanula white and blue, with abundance of lovely tinted deep orange potentills and rich carmine dianthus, were growing at our feet, with numerous other wild flowers. The pretty pink mallow, cultivated in gardens, grows everywhere, but not so luxuriantly here as about Morteau, and the serviceberry and barberry have almost disappeared. This is indeed a paradise for botanists, but their travels should be made earlier in the year. The walks and drives in the neighbourhood of Besancon are countless, but that to the little valley of the. World's End, "Le Bout du Monde," must on no account be omitted.

Again we follow the limpid waters of the winding Doubs; on one side hanging vineyards and orchards, on the other lines of poplars, above these dimpled green

---

2 "Oppidum maximum Sequauorum, natura loci, sic muniebatur ut magnam ad ducendum bellum daret facultatem: propterea quod flumen Dubis ut circino circumductum, pene totum oppidum cingit; reliquum spatium [quod non est amplius pedum DC. qua flumen intermittit,] mons continet magna altitudine, ita ut radices ejus montis ex utra parte ripae fluminis continguat." De Bello Gallico, Lib. I., chap, xxxviii. A marvellous bit of accurate description this, and to be commended to writers of guide-books.

hills and craggy peaks are reflected in the still transparent water. We reach the pretty village of Beurre after a succession of landscapes, "l'un plus joli que l'autre," as our French neighbours say, and then come suddenly upon a tiny valley shut in by lofty rocks, aptly called the World's End of these parts, since here the most adventuresome pedestrian must retrace his steps--no possibility of scaling these mountain-walls, from which a cascade falls so musically; no outlet from these im- pregnable walls into the pastoral country on the other side. We must go back by the way we have come, first having penetrated to the heart of the valley by a winding path, and watched the silvery waters tumble down from the grey rocks that seem to touch the blue sky overhead.

The great charm of these landscapes is the abundance of water to be found everywhere, and no less delightful is the sight of springs, fountains, and pumps in every village. Besancon is noted for its handsome fountains, some of which are real works of art, but the tiniest hamlets in the neighbourhood, and, indeed, throughout the whole department of the Doubs, are as well supplied as the city itself. We know what an aristocratic luxury good water is in many an English village, and how too often the poor have no pure drinking water within reach at all; here they have close at hand enough and to spare of the purest and best, and not only their share of that, but of the good things of the earth as well, a bit of vegetable and fruit-garden, a vineyard, and, generally speaking, a little house of their own. Here, as a rule, ev- erybody possesses something, and the working watchmakers have, most of them, their suburban gardens, to which they resort on Sundays and holidays. Besancon is very rich in suburban retreats, and nothing can be more enticing than the cottages and villas nestled so cosily along the vine-clad hills that surround it on every side. It is, above all, rich in public walks and promenades, one of these, the Promenade Chamart--a corruption of Champ de Mars--possessing some of the finest plane trees in Europe--a gigantic bit of forest on the verge of this city--of wonderful beauty and stateliness. These veteran trees vary in height from thirty to thirty-five yards. The Promenade Micaud, so called after its originator, Mayor of Besancon, in 1842, winds along the river-side, and affords lovely views at every turn. Then there are so-called "squares" in the heart of the town, where military bands play twice a week, and nursemaids and their charges spend the afternoons. Perhaps no city of its size in all France, Besancon numbers only sixty thousand inhabitants, is better off in this respect, whilst it is so enriched by vine-clad hills and mountains that the country peeps in everywhere.

Considered from all points of view it is a very attractive place to live in, and possesses all the resources of the capital on a small scale; an excellent theatre, free art schools, and an academy of arts, literary, scientific and artistic societies, museums, picture galleries, lastly, one of the finest public libraries in France, of which a word or two more later on. First of all something must be said of the city itself, which is especially interesting to the archaeologist and historian, and is very little frequented by English tourists. Alternately Roman, Burgundian, Arlesian, Anglo-French, and Spanish, Besancon has seen extraordinary vicissitudes. In the twelfth century it was constituted a free city or Commune, and was not incorporated into the French kingdom till the reign of Louis XIV. Traces of these various occupations remain, and as we enter in at one gate and pass out of another, we have each successive chapter of its history suggested to us in the noble Porte Noire or Roman triumphal arch; the ancient cathedral first forming a Roman basilica; the superb semi-Italian, semi-Spanish Palais Granvelle, the Hotel-de-Ville with its handsome sixteenth century facade; the Renaissance council chamber in magnificently carved oak of the Palais de Justice--all these stamp the city with the seal of different epochs, and lend majesty to the modern, handsome town into which the Besancon of former times has been transformed. The so-called Porte Taillee a Roman gate hewn out of the solid rock, forms an imposing entry to the city, the triumphal arch before mentioned leading to the Cathedral only. Here most picturesquely stand the columns and other fragments of the Roman theatre excavated by the learned librarian, M. Castan, a few years back. The Archbishop allows no one to see the art-treasures contained in the archiepiscopal palace, among which is a fine Paul Veronese; but the Cathedral is fortunately open, and there the art-lovers may rejoice in perhaps one of the most beautiful Fra Bartolomeos in the world, unfortunately hung too high to be well seen. Exteriorly the Cathedral offers little interest, but the interior is very gorgeous--a dazzling display of gold ornaments, stained glass, pictures, mosaics, and ecclesiastical riches of all kinds. The other churches of Besancon are not interesting, architecturally speaking, though picturesque, especially St. Pierre, with its clock-tower conspicuously seen from every part of the town. The archaeological museum is considered the best arranged, as also, in some respects, it is the richest in France, and contains some wonderfully beautiful things, notably the Celtic collection found at Alaise, in the Department of the Jura--supposed by some authorities to be the Alesia of Julius Caesar, whilst others have decided in favour of Alise Sainte Reine, in Auvergne, where a statue has been raised to the noble Vercingetorix. There are also Gallo-Roman objects of great interest and beauty collected from Mandeure (Epanuoduorum) and other parts of Franche-Comte. Such collections must be studied in detail to be appreciated, and I only mention them as affording another illustration of the principle of decentralization carried on in France--each city and town being enriched and embellished, as far as possible, and made a centre artistic, scientific, and literary. The museum contains amongst other things a curious collection of old watches, the speciality of Besancon, of which more will be said hereafter. But what was my astonishment and delight, as I sauntered by the little cases under the window containing coins, medals, and antiquities of various kinds, to come suddenly upon a label bearing the inscription:--

"La Montre de Vergniaud."

There it lay, the little gold watch of the great Girondin orator, choicest, most precious relic of the Revolution, historic memento unrivalled for interest and romantic associations! Vergniaud's watch! The very words take one's breath away, yet there it was, close under my eyes. All those of my readers who are well acquainted with the history of the Revolution in detail, will remember the Last Banquet of the Girondins, that memorable meeting together of the martyrs of liberty, each one condemned to die next morning for his political creed. The Girondins ruthlessly swept away, the last barrier removed between principle and passion, and the Revolutionary tide was free to work destruction at its will; of these, Vergniaud was undoubtedly the greatest, and anything and everything connected with him has a magic interest. After the banquet, which was held with much state and ceremony in a hall of the Conciergerie, now shown to travellers, the twenty-seven Girondins discoursed in Platonic fashion upon the subjects nearest their hearts, namely, the future of Republican ideas and the immortality of the soul. This solemn symposium brought to an end, each occupied himself differently, some in making their last testament, others in deep thought, one in calm sleep; and it was during the interval

that Vergniaud with a pin scratched inside the case of his elegant little gold watch
the name of Adele, and having done this he handed it to a trustworthy gaoler to
be delivered next day. A few hours later his head had fallen on the guillotine, but
his last request was duly delivered to the Adele for whom he designed it, a little
girl of thirteen who was to have become his wife. She became in due time a happy
wife and mother, and bequeathed Vergniaud's historic watch to a friend, who generously bestowed it upon the Besancon Museum. Charles Nodier, in his "Dernier
Banquet des Girondins," gives an eloquent history of this watch, which most likely
he saw and handled as a youth. Vergniaud is undoubtedly one of the most striking
and imposing figures in the Revolution, and everything concerning him is of deepest interest. His lofty soul, no more than any other of that epoch, could foresee how
the French Republic would be established peaceably and friendly after torrents of
blood and crimes and errors unspeakable.

The picture-galleries, arranged in fine handsome rooms adjoining, contain several chefs d'oeuvre amid a fairly representative collection of French art. The fine
Albert Duerer--an altarpiece in wood--the Moro portraits, the Bronzino--Descent
from the Cross--all veritable gems, lastly the portrait of Cardinal Granvelle by Titian. This is a noble work; there are also two canvases attributed to Velasquez,
"Galileo," and a "Mathematician." Seeing that Besancon was under Spanish pro-
tection during the great painter's lifetime, and that all kinds of art-treasures were
amassed by the Granvelles in their superb palace, it might well happen that works
of Velasquez should have found their way here. Authorities must decide on the
genuineness of these two real works of art.

Under the same roof is the free art-school for students of both sexes, which is
one of the most flourishing institutes of the town, and dates from the year 1794. In
the second year of study, drawing is taught from the living model, and every facility
is thus afforded to those unable to pursue their studies in Paris, or pay the expense
of a private study. There is also a free music-school and technical schools, both
gratuitous, and open to both sexes. Nor must we forget the Academy of Science and
Belles Lettres, which not only affords complete scientific and literary instruction
gratuitously to the poor student, but also courses of lectures open to the general
public from October till June. These lectures may be compared to the Winter series of our Royal Institution, (alas! the privilege of the rich and at least well-to-do

only!) and, besides offering a rare intellectual treat to lovers of science and letters generally, are of the greatest possible use to needy students. Indeed, so liberal is the City of Besancon in this respect that any lad who has been lucky enough to get a nomination to the Lycee, may here pass his examination for the Bachelier-es-Lettres and es-Science without a farthing of costs. Again I may remark, as far as I know, no English town of 60,000 inhabitants, more or less, offers anything like the same advantages in the matter of higher instruction to those who cannot afford to pay for it; but perhaps my English critics will reply that those who cannot pay the cost of Royal Institution or other lectures are unreasonable to expect scientific instruction, or recreation, to which argument I have nothing to say. The fact remains, as everyone who lives in France knows well enough, that we have nothing to be compared to the free Academies, free art and music schools found there so largely, and which have received considerable development of late years. Many of these date from the great Revolution, when the highest instruction was not considered too good for the people. The superior taste, technical skill, and general intelligence of French workmen are due to those causes, and, of course, chiefly to the accessibility of museums, libraries, art-collections, &c. on Sundays. No matter which of these you may happen to visit on a Sunday, you are sure to find that soldiers, artisans and peasants curiously inspecting the treasures displayed to view--even dry geological and archaeological collections attracting their attention. It is impossible to have anything to do with the French working classes, and not observe the effect of this artistic culture, and here and there throughout this work I have adduced instances in point. We have nothing in England to be compared to the general filtration of artistic ideas, by means of gratuitous art and technical instruction, and the opening on Sunday of all art and literary collections.

But after all it is the watchmaking school, or, Ecole d'Horlogerie that will perhaps most interest and instruct the traveller here, and he should by no means neglect to visit it; however short his stay may be. Watchmaking is, as is well known, the speciality of Besancon, and dates as an important branch of industry from the year 1793. The National Convention is to be thanked for the foundation of the first "horlogerie," having invited to Besancon the refugee watchmakers of Chaux de Fonds and Locle, who had been prescribed for their adherence to the Republican idea. By a decree of the Convention, these exiles were accorded succour, after which the Committee declared watchmaking in the Department of the Doubs to be a national institution. Many hundred thousand watches are made here annually, and it has been computed that, out of every hundred watches in the French market, eighty-six come from Besancon. In the year 1873, 353,764 watches were made, representing a capital of fifteen millions of francs, and the trade increases annually. The watchmaking school located in the picturesque old Grenier, or public granary of the city, numbers over a hundred pupils of both sexes, and is of course gratuitous. The Besancon watches are noted for their elegance and cheapness, being sold at prices which would surprise eminent London watchmakers. Many working watchmakers on a small scale, are here, who, by dint of great economy, contrive to purchase a bit of garden and summer house outside the town, whither they go on Sundays and holidays to breathe the fresh air, and cultivate their flowers and vegetables. But the majority are capitalists on a large scale, as at Montbeliard, and I fear the workman's hours here are as long as at the latter place. The length of the day's labour in France is appalling, the one blot on a bright picture of thrift, independence, and a general well-being.

Delightful hours may be spent in the Public Library, one of the richest of provincial France, which is also, like the charming little library of Weimar, a museum as well. The most superb of these bibliographical treasures were amassed by the Keeper of the Seals of Charles the Fifth, Perrenot de Granvelle, and afterwards bequeathed by the Abbe Brisot, into whose possession they had fallen, to the town of Besancon. Among them are some splendid manuscripts from the library of Mathias Corvinus, King of Hungary, and a vast collection of choice Aldines bound in the costliest manner. No less than 1,200 volumes of the sixteenth century are here, amongst these several specimens of topography printed in Franche-Comte. Lovers of rare MSS., old books, and old bindings, have here a feast, indeed, and are generously allowed access to all. Like most other important, libraries in France, it is under the management of a man of learning and distinction; M. Castan, the present librarian, is the author of some valuable works relating to his native province and to his archaeological labours. Besancon is mainly indebted not only for the excavations, which have filled its museums with treasures, but for the imposing Roman remains which adorn its streets. Besides its bibliographical collections, the library contains a vast number of coins, medallions, busts, engravings, and portraits relating to the history of Franche-Comte, many of which are highly interesting. The busts, portraits, and relics of such noble Franc-Comtois as have won a European reputation--George Cuvier, for instance, whose brain weighed more than that of any human being ever known; Victor Hugo, whose works are familiar to readers in all languages; Charles Fourier, who saw in the Phalanstery, or, Associated Home, a remedy for the crying social evils of the age, and who, in spite of many aberrations, is entitled to the gratitude of mankind for his efforts on behalf of education, and the elevation of the laborious classes; Proudhon, whose famous dictum, "La propriete c'est le vol," has become the watchword of a certain school of Socialists, which even the iron despotism of Russia and Germany cannot keep down; Charles Nodier, charming litterateur, who, at the age of twenty-one, was the author of the first satire ever published against the first Napoleon, "La Napoleone," which formulated the indignation of the Republican party, and a noble roll-call of artists, authors, savants, soldiers, and men of science.

Noteworthy in this treasure-house of Franc-Comtois history is the fine marble statue of Jouffroy by Pradier. Jouffroy, of whom his native province may well be proud, disputes with Fulton the honour of first having applied steam to the purposes of navigation. His efforts, made on the river Doubs and the Saone in 1776 and 1783, failed for the want of means to carry out his ideas in full, but the Academy of Science acknowledged his claim to the discovery in 1840. The Besancon Library, indeed, whether considered as such pur et simple, or a museum, is full of interest and instruction, and deserves a lengthened visit. The collection of works on art, architecture, and archaeology bequeathed to the city by Paris, architect and designer to Louis XVI., is a very rich one and there is also a cabinet of medals numbering ten thousand pieces.

Besancon also boasts of several learned societies, one of which founded in the interests of scientific inquiry so far back as 1840, "La Societe d'Emulation du Doubs," numbers five hundred and odd members. One of the most interesting features in the ancient city is its connection with Spain, and what has been termed the golden age of Franche-Comte under the Emperor Charles the Fifth. It will be remembered that Franche-Comte formed a part of the dowry of Margaret, daughter of the Emperor Maximilian of Austria, and it was under her protectorate during her life-time and reverted to her nephew Charles the Fifth on his accession to the crowns of Spain,

Austria, the Low Countries, and Burgundy. His minister, Perrenot de Granvelle, born at Ornans, infused new intellectual and artistic life into the place he ruled as a prince. His stately Italian palace, still one of the handsomest monuments of Besancon, was filled with pictures, statues, books, and precious manuscripts, and the stimulus thus given to literature and the fine arts was followed by a goodly array of artists, thinkers, and writers. The learned Gilbert Cousin, secretary of Erasmus, Prevost, pupil of Raffaelle, Goudinel of Besancon, the master of Palestrina, creator of popular music, the lettered family of Chifflet, and many others, shed lustre on this splendid period; while not only Besancon but Lons-le-Saunier, Arbois, and other small towns bear evidence of Spanish influence on architecture and the arts. In the most out of the way places may be found chefs-d'oeuvre dating from the protectorate of Margaret and the Emperor, and it is such scattered treasure-trove that makes travelling in out of the way places in Franche-Comte so fruitful to the art-lover in various fields.

The most salient feature of social life at Besancon is its Catholicism, the place literally swarming with priests, and soldiers, to the great detriment of public morality. The Protestants, nevertheless, hold their own here, and even gain ground, witness the Protestant Church established within the last ten years at Arbois by the Consistory of Besancon. They have also succeeded in founding a hospital here for the sick and aged poor, which is the greatest possible boon. Up till that time, this section of the community had been received in the municipal hospital under the management of the nuns, who, of course, did all in their power to worry their patients into Catholicism. We know what happens when a hospital is under the charge of nuns, and it can easily be understood that many of these poor people preferred to embrace a crucifix than forego their broth when half dead of exhaustion. Some would go through a mock conversion, others would endure a martyrdom till the last; but the position alike of weak and obstinate was unbearable. Now there is a home, not only for the indigent sick and aged, but for those who can afford to pay a small sum for being well looked after; and it is delightful to witness the home-like ease and comfort everywhere. The poor people welcomed their pastor, who accompanied me on my visit, not only as a priest but as a friend, and it was easy to see how they enjoyed a little talk with Madame, and the prattle of the children.

The large shady hospital garden overlooking the town is much resorted to in fine weather, and everywhere we found cheerful faces. It is hardly necessary to say that this admirable work needs money. The Catholic clergy, of course, regard any step in advance on the part of the Protestants with abhorrence, and do a little bit of persecution whenever opportunity offers. Thus, as perhaps may not be known to all my readers, the parish burial-ground in France is open by the law to all sects and denominations indiscriminately; Protestant, Jew, Mahometan, or Brahmin may here find a resting-place in spite of M. le Cure. Such is the law, and an admirable law it is, but the law means one thing to a Catholic and another to a Protestant There is no Protestant burial-ground in Besancon or the neighbouring villages, so that everyone is buried in the town and parish cemetery; but, as mayors of small country towns and villages often happen not to know the law, the cure tries to circumvent his enemy at the last. Accordingly, when the time of burial comes, a Protestant pastor may be kept waiting for hours in consequence of this wilful ob-stinacy; supposing that the mayor is under clerical influence, useless to argue "La loi est avec nous;" cure and mayor persist, and at the last moment the unfortunate pastor has to telegraph to the Prefet, who, whether clerical or not, knows the law, and is obliged to follow it, and consequently sends an authorization which ends the matter. This is very blind on the part of the clericals, for it naturally turns the Prot-estants into martyrs. It happened in a little village, not far from Besancon, that, after a scene of this kind, all the village population turned into the cemetery, and, by the time the Prefet's order came, the Protestant pastor had a large audience for his discourse over the grave. "C'est si consolant chez les Protestants, l'enterrement des morts," people were heard to say, and let us hope that the cure and the mayor were punished for their folly by a few conversions among their flocks to Protestantism.

A mediaeval writer, Francois de Belleforest, thus describes Besancon:--

"Si par l'antiquite, continuee en grandeur, la benediction de Dieu se cognoit en une lieu, il n'y a ville ni cite en toutes les Gaules qui ayt plus grande occasion de remarquer la faveur de Dieu, en soy que la cite dont nous avions prise le discours. Car, en premier lieu, elle est assise en aussi bonne et riche assiette que ville du monde; estant entoure de riches costeaux et vignobles, et de belles et hautes forets, ayant la riviere du Doux qui passe par le millieu, et enclost pour le plupart d'icelle, estant bien, d'ailleurs fort bien approvisionee. Les fruicts y sont aussi bons, et y a aussi bonne commodite de venaison et de gibier en ceste ville, qu'en autre qu'on sceut choisir. Et puis ce qu'elle est a la cheultes des montagnes, on la tient pour le grenier commun du comte de Bourgogne, comme jadis Sicile estait de l'Itaile. Et s'il etait question d'estimer la vertu d'un peuple, qui s'est longtemps maintenu libre sans ployer la gantelet, ni rien perdu de sa reputation, on peut, a bon droit, faire cas de ceste cite. Et certes de tout temps ceste brave cite a este enviee des tyrans, pour en usurper la domination. Et il n'y a ni eu ni menaces, ni allechement qui ayent sceu esbranler les nobles et libres coeurs besanconnais, pour quicter aucune chose de leurs libertez, quelques couleurs de grandeur et de richesses qu'on leur ayt mis audevant pour se laisser annexer au comte de Bourgogne, et avoir un parlement, et se mettre auxpieds ce qu'il ont aux mains."

CHAPTER VII
ORNANS, COURBET'S COUNTRY,
AND THE VALLEY OF THE LOUE.

Let the reader now follow me to Ornans, Courbet's birth and favourite abiding place, and the lovely Valley of the Loue. This is the excursion par excellence from Besancon, and may be made in two ways, either on foot, occupying three or four days, decidedly the most advantageous for those who can do it, or by carriage in a single day, starting very early in the morning, and telegraphing for relays at Ornans the previous afternoon. This is how we managed it, starting at five, and reaching home soon after eight at night. The children accompanied us, and I must say, better fellow-travellers I never had than these mites of sixteen months and three and a-half years. When tired of looking at the cows, oxen, goats, horses and poultry, we passed on the road, they would amuse themselves for an hour by quietly munching a roll, and, when that occupation at last came to an end, they would go to sleep, waking up just as happy as before.

Here I will mention that the great amiability of the French character is no more strongly manifested than in this habit of always having their little children about them. As neither day nor night nurseries exist in France, and head-nurses are equally unheard of, young children are always with their parents. Thus, if visitors call, and papa and mamma happen to be engaged in interesting conversation with them, no attention will be paid to the perpetual noise and interruption of little toddling things, whose place is naturally there. I have heard an animated political discussion go on whilst a boy of two and a half was hammering with a hammer on a wooden box; and no kind of notice was taken by his elders. Such a practice, of course, could only be made tolerable by excessive good-nature, but there is no doubt that our own system is better both for parents and children.

Ornans is not only extremely picturesque in itself, but interesting as the birth and favourite abiding place of the famous painter Courbet; it is also a starting place for the Valley of the Loue, and the source of this beautiful little river, the last only to be seen in fine, dry weather, on account of the steepness and slipperiness of the road. The climate of Franche-Comte is unfortunately very much like our own, being excessively changeable, rainy, blowy, sunny, all in a breath. To-day's unclouded sunshine is no guarantee of fine weather to-morrow, and although, as a rule, September is the finest month of the year here, it was very variable during my stay, with alternations of rain and chilliness. Fine days had to be waited for and seized upon with avidity, whilst the temperature is liable to great and sudden variations.

Ornans we reach after a drive of three hours, amid hills luxuriantly draped with vines and craggy peaks clothed with verdure, here and there wide sketches of velvety green pasture with cattle feeding, haymakers turning over the autumn hay. Everywhere we find haymakers at work, and picturesque figures they are.

Ornans is lovely, and no wonder that Courbet was so fond of it. Nestled in a deep valley of green rocks and vineyards, and built on the banks of the transparent Loue, its quaint spire rising from the midst, it commends itself alike to artist, naturalist, and angler. These old-world houses reflected in the river are marvellously paintable, and the scene, as we saw it after a heavy rain, glowed in the brightest and warmest light.

Courbet's house is situated, not on the river, but by the roadside, on the outskirts of the town, fronting the river and the bright green terraced hills above. It is a low, one-storied house, embosomed in greenery, very rural, pretty, and artistic. In the dining-room we were shown a small statue of the painter by his own hand, giving one rather the idea of a country-squire or sporting farmer than a great artist, and his house--which is not shown to strangers--is full of interesting reminiscences of its owner. In the kitchen is a splendid Renaissance chimney-piece in sculptured marble, fit for the dining-hall of a Rothschild. This, Courbet found in some old chateau near, and, artist-like, transferred it to his cottage. On the walls of the studio are two frescoes he painted in his happier days, before he helped to overthrow the Vendome Column, and thus forfeited the good feeling of his fellow-townsmen. Ornans is clerical to the backbone, and will it be believed?--after this unfortunate affair of the Vendome Column, an exquisite statue, with which Courbet had decorated the public fountain, was thrown down, of course at clerical instigation. Morteau, it must be supposed, being more enlightened, rescued the dishonoured statue, and it now adorns the public fountain of that village. It is, indeed, impossible to give any idea of the vindictive spirit with which poor Courbet was treated by his native village, and, seeing how much he loved it, it must have galled him deeply. We were allowed to wander at will over the house and straggling gardens, having friends in the present occupants, but the house still belongs to the Courbet family, and is not otherwise to be seen.

All this time I was listening, with no little edification, to the remarks of our young driver, who took the keenest interest in Courbet and art generally. He told me, as an instance of the strong feeling existing against Courbet after the events of the Commune, that, upon one occasion when the painter had been drinking a toast with a friend in a cafe, he had no sooner quitted the place than a young officer sprang up and dashed the polluted glass to the ground, shattering it into a dozen pieces. "No one shall henceforth drink out of a glass used by that man," he said, and doubtless he was only echoing the popular sentiment.

Ornans is the birthplace of the princely Perronet de Granvelle (father of the Cardinal whose portrait by Titian adorns the picture-gallery of Besancon), and whose munificent patronage of arts and letters turned that city into a little Florence during the Spanish regime. In the church is seen the plain red marble sarcophagus of his parents, also a carved reading desk and several pictures presented to the church by his son, the Cardinal. There is a curious old Spanish house in the town, a relic of the same epoch. Ornans is celebrated for its cherry orchards and fabrications of Kirsch, also for Absinthe, and its wines. Everywhere you see cherry orchards and artificial terraces for the vines as on the Rhine, not a ledge of hill side being wasted. Gruyere cheese, so called, is also made here, and there are besides several manufactures, nail-forges, wire-drawing mills, and tile-kilns. But none of these interfere with the pastoralness of the scenery, and no wonder that this attracts French artists in the summer time. Lovely walks and drives abound, and the magnificence of the forest trees has been made familiar to us by the landscapes of Courbet, whose name will ever be associated with this quaint village in the Valley of the Loue.

We are now on the high road from Ornans to Pontarlier, and are passing some of the wealthiest little communities in Franche-Comte, Montgesoye, Vuillafans, Lods, all most picturesque to behold, and important centres of industry. Iron foundries, kirsch distilleries, chemical works, and other manufactures maintain these rustic populations, and such isolated little nuclei of trade will doubtless take extraordinary development when the line of railway from Besancon to Pontarlier, by way of Ornans, is completed. At present it is one of the few places that may be described as out of the world, and a veritable paradise for the lover of quiet and rusticity. If we proceed further on the Monthier road, the aspect changes, and we find ourselves in the winding close-shut valley, the narrow turbulent little streams of deepest green tossing over its rocky bed amid hanging vineyards and lofty cliffs. Soon, however, the vine, the oak, the beech, and the ash tree disappear, and we have instead the sombre pine and fir only.

Monthier is perched on a hill-side amid grandiose mountains, and is hardly less picturesque than Ornans, though not nearly so enticing. In fact it is a trifle dirty when visited in detail, though charming, viewed from the high road above. Here we sat down to an excellent dinner at one end of the salle-a-manger; at the other was a long table where a number of peasant farmers, carters, and graziers--it was fair day--were faring equally well: our driver was amongst them, and all were as quiet and well-behaved as possible, but given to spit on the floor, "as is their nature to." The charges were very low, the food good, the wine sour as vinegar, and the people obliging in the extreme. The hotels in these parts are very much on a par with caravanserais in Algeria; bells, fire-places, and other necessities of civilized life are unknown, the bed-rooms are often reached by an outside staircase only, and afford such accommodation we should not think luxurious for a stable-boy in England, and these often, moreover, adjoin a noisy upper salle-a-manger, where eating, and drinking, and talking go on all day long.

After having stopped to look at the beautiful old wood carvings in the church, we continue our way, climbing the mountain road towards Pontarlier; hardly knowing which to admire most, the deep-lying valley at our feet, where the little imprisoned river curls with a noise as of thunder, making miniature cascades at every step, or the limestone rocks of majestic shape towering above on the other side. One of them, the so-called Roche de Hautepierre, is nearly nine hundred yards high; the road all the time zigzags wonderfully around the mountain sides, a stupendous piece of engineering which cost the originator his life. Soon after passing the tunnel cut in the rock, we saw an inscription telling how the engineer, while engaged in taking his measurements, lost his footing and was precipitated into the awful ravine below. The road itself was opened in 1845, and is mainly due to the public spirit of the inhabitants of Ornans.

Franche-Comte is rich in zig-zagging mountain roads of daring construction, and none are more wonderful than this. As we crawl at a snail's pace between rocks and ravine, silvery grey masses towering against the glowing purple sky, deepest green fastnesses below that make us giddy to behold, all is still but for the sea-like war of the little river as it pours down impetuously from its mountain home. The heavy rain of the previous night unfortunately prevents us from following it to its source, a delightful excursion in tolerably dry weather, but impracticable after a rain-fall. By far the best, way is to sleep at Monthier and visit the source on foot, but fatigue may be avoided by taking a carriage from Pontarlier. Between Monthier and the source of the Loue is a bit of wild romantic scenery known as the Combes de Nouaille, home of the Franc-Comtois elf, or fairy, called la Vouivre. Combe, it must be explained, means a straight, narrow valley lying between two mountains, and Charles Nodier remarks: "is very French, and is perfectly intelligible in any part of the country, but has been omitted in the Dictionary of the Academy, because there is no combe at the Tuileries, the Champs Elysees or the Luxembourg!" These close winding combes form one of the most characteristic and picturesque features of Franc-Comtois scenery. Leaving the more adventuresome part of this journey therefore to travellers luckier in respect of weather than ourselves, we turn our horses' heads towards Ornans, where we rest for coffee and a little chat with friends. As we set out for Besancon, a splendid glow of sunset lights up Courbet's birth and favourite abiding place, clothing in richest gold the hills and hanging woods he portrayed with so much vigour and poetic feeling. The glories of the sinking sun lingered long, and, when the last crimson rays faded, a full pearly moon rose in the clear heavens, lighting us on our way.

A few days after this delightful excursion, I left Besancon, as I had done Montbeliard, amid the heartiest leave-takings, and the last recollection I brought away from the venerable town is of two little fair-haired boys, whose faces were lifted to mine for a farewell kiss in the railway station.

CHAPTER VIII.
SALINS, ARBOIS, AND THE WINE COUNTRY OF THE JURA.

Hardly has the traveller quitted Besancon in the direction of Lons-le-Saunier ere he finds himself amid wholly different scenery; all is now on a bolder, vaster scale, desolate sweeps of rocky plain, shelving mountain sides, bits of scant herbage alternating with vineyards, the golden foliage lending wondrous lustre to the otherwise arid landscapes, the rocks rising higher and higher as we go--such are the features that announce the Jura. We have left the gentler beauties of the Doubs behind us, and are now in one of the most romantic and picturesque regions of all France. Salins, perhaps the only cosmopolitan town that the Jura can be said to possess, since hither English and other tourists flock in the summer season, is superbly situated--a veritable fairy princess guarded by monster dragons! Four tremendous mountain peaks protect it on every side, towering above the little town with imposing aspect; and it is no less strongly defended by art, each of these mountain tops being crested with fortifications. Salins bears indeed a formidable front to the enemy, and no wonder the Prussians could not take it. Strategically, of course, its position is most important, as a glance at the map will show. It is in itself a wonderful little place from its "assiette," as the French say; and wherever you go you find wild natural beauty, while the brisk mountain air is delightful to breathe, and the transparent atmosphere lends an extra glow to every feature of the scene.

At Salins too we find ourselves in a land of luxuries, i.e., clean floors, chambermaids, bells, sofas, washing basins and other items in hygiene and civilization not worth mentioning. The Hotel des Messageries is very pleasant, and here, as in the more primitive regions before described, you are received rather as a guest to be made much of than as a foreigner to be imposed upon. This charming bonhomie, found among all classes, is apt to take the form of gossip overmuch, which is sometimes wearisome. The Franc-Comtois, I must believe, are the greatest talkers in the world, and any chance listener to be caught by the button is not easily let go. Yet a considerable amount of volubility is pardoned when people are so amiable and obliging.

Mendicity is forbidden in the Jura as in the Department of the Doubs, and there is little real pinching poverty to be found among the rural population, though of course a laboriousness and economy unknown among our own. In the most part, the vine-grower and fabricator of Gruyere cheese, so called, is well-to-do and independent, and here indeed, the soil is the property of the people.

The Salins season ends on the 15th of September, when the magnificent hydropathic establishment is closed, and only a few stray visitors remain. The Salins waters are said to be much more efficacious than those of Kreuznach in Prussia, which they much resemble; and the nature of the soil is shown by its deep crimson hue. If the tonic qualities of these mountain springs are invaluable, it must be admitted that they are done ample justice to, for never surely were so many public fountains to be found in a town of the same size. A charming monograph might be devoted to the public fountains of Franche-Comte, and those of Salins are especially meritorious as works of art. How many there are, I cannot say, but at least half-a-dozen are interesting as monuments, notably the charming life-size bronze figure of a Vintager, by the gifted Salinois sculptor, Max Claudel, ornamenting one, the fine torso surmounting another, and of which the history is mysterious, the group of swans adorning a third, and so on; at every turn the stranger coming upon some street ornament of this kind, whilst the perpetual sound of running water is delightful to the ear. I shall never recall the Jura without this cool, pleasant, dripping noise, as much a part of it as its brisk air and dazzling blue sky.

There is a good deal to see at Salins; the salines, or salt-works, the old church of St. Anatole with its humorous wood-carvings, the exquisite Bruges tapestries in the Museum, the ancient gateways of the city, the quaint Renaissance statue of St. Maurice in the church of that name--wooden figure of a soldier-peasant on horseback--and lastly the forts and the superb panoramas to be obtained from them. This little straggling town, of not more than six thousand and odd inhabitants, possesses a public library of ten thousand volumes, a natural history museum, and a theatre, and other resources. It is eminently Catholic, but I was glad to find that the thin edge of the Protestant wedge is being driven in there, a Protestant service being now held once a month, and this will doubtless soon develop into some regular organization. Protestantism means cleanliness, education, and domestic morality, and Catholicism the reverse; so no wonder that the more enlightened mayors and municipalities are inclined to look upon these quiet invasions with favour. As I narrate my progress through the Jura, it will be seen that I found Protestantism everywhere making head against the enemy.

Perhaps the most beautiful excursion to be made from Salins is to the little town of Nans, and the source of the River Lison, a two hours' drive amid scenery of alternating loveliness and grandeur--vines everywhere as we climb upwards, our road curling round the mountain-sides, as a ribbon twisted round a sugar-loaf, and then having wound in and out jagged peaks covered with light foliage and abrupt slopes clad with vines, we come to the sombre pine-forests, passing from one forest to another, the air blowing upon us with sudden keenness. No sooner do we emerge from these gloomy precincts than we come upon the pretty little village of Nans, smiling and glowing in a warm sunlit valley, and most enticing to us after the sombreness and chilliness of the mountain-tops.

Although anything but a gourmand myself, I will mention for the benefit of those who really care for good things, that we found a most wonderful dinner awaiting us in the homely little auberge at which we alighted--hare, salmon, trout, prawns, and all kinds of local confectionery, were here supplied at the modest price of ten francs and a half, the cook of the establishment being the landlady herself, and the entire staff consisting of two old women. One of these was drafted off to guide me to the source, and off we set on our walk, at once leaving the warm open valley for the mountain world. On and on we went, the mountain closing upon us and shutting out more and more of the glowing blue heavens, till we came to a stand. From these rocky fastnesses, here forbidding further progress, the River Lison has its source; above they show a silvery grey surface against the emerald of the valleys and the sapphire of the sky, but below the huge clefts, from which we are soon to see the river issue forth exultingly, they are black as night.

A few steps onward and we were in sight of the source, and no words can convey its imposingness, or the sense of contrast forced upon the mind--the pitchy, ebon cavern from which flashes the river in silvery whiteness, tumbling in a dozen cascades down glistening black rocks, and across pebbly beds, and along gold-green pastures. We explored the inner part of this strange rock-bed; the little River Lison, springing from its dark cavernous home, leaping forth with wild exultation into the light, pursuing its way under all kinds of difficulties, growing broader and broader as it goes, till a wide, sunlit river, it flows onward and onward, finally reaching the sea, reminded me, as I gazed, of a lovely thought emerging from the thinker's brain, which, after obstacles and hindrances innumerable, at last, refreshing all as it goes, reaches the open light of universal truth.

Behind the source, and reached by a winding path cut in the rocks, is a lofty chasm, from the summit of which another mountain stream falls with beautiful effect; and no less impressive and curious are the so-called Grottes des Sarrazins, a little further off, huge caverns shutting in a little lake, and where the river rushes with a sound of thunder.

On the steep mountain path, leading to the chasm just mentioned, we found hellebore growing in abundance, also the winter-cherry, its vermillion-hued capsules glowing through the green. The brilliant red berry of the white bream-tree also lends colour to the wayside hedge, as well as the deep rose-coloured fruit of the barberry. Flowers also grow in abundance; and in the town their cultivation seems a passion. Some gardens contain sun-flowers, or little else, others are full of zinnias, flowering mallow trees, and balsams. There is no gardening aimed at, in our sense of the word, but simply abundance of colour; the flowers are planted anyhow and grow anyhow, the result being ornamental in the extreme.

There is a pottery, or faiencerie; of two hundred years standing at Nans, and some of the wares are very pretty and artistic. The chief characteristics of the Nans ware, or cailloutage, is its creamy, highly-glazed surface, on which are painted, by hand, flowers, birds, and arabesques in brilliant colours, and in more or less elaborate styles. Attempts are also made to imitate the well-known Strasburg ware, of which great quantities are found in these parts, chiefly at sales in old houses. The Strasburg ware is known by its red flowers--chiefly roses and tulips--on a creamy ground, also elaborate arabesques in deep purple. If we take up a specimen, we find the ornamentation done at random, and, in fact, the artist was compelled to this method of working in order to conceal the imperfections of the porcelain. The Nans ware--very like the faiencerie of Salins--commends itself alike for form and design, and the working potters employed there will be found full of information, which they are very ready to impart. One of them, with whom I fell into conversation, had just returned from the Paris Exhibition, and expressed himself with enthusiasm concerning the English ceramic galleries, of which, indeed, we may be proud.

It is impossible to exaggerate the beauty of Salins, and its stately environment of rock and vine-clad peak, especially seen on such a September day as this I describe, when the sky is of warmest blue, and the air so transparent, fresh, and exhilarating that merely to breathe is a pleasure. Nor are the people less striking than their mountain home. Dark hair, rich complexions, regular features, an animated expression, are the portion of most, especially of the women, whilst all wear a look of cheerfulness and health. No rags, no poverty, no squalor; and the abundance of natural resources brings the good things of life within reach of all. At the unpretending hotel, the cookery would not discredit the Hotel de Bristol itself, everything being of the best. I was served with a little bird which I ate with great innocence, and no little relish, supposing it to be a snipe, but, on asking what it was, I found, to my horror, the wretches had served up a thrush! I am sorry to say a tremendous slaughter of migratory birds goes on at this time of the year; not only thrushes, but larks, linnets, and other sweet little songsters supplying the general dinner table. The thrushes feed largely on grapes, which lend them a delicious flavour when cooked, and for which nefarious practice on their part they are said to be destroyed. I was assured that a thrush will eat two bunches of grapes a day, and so they are killed by the hundreds of thousands, and sold for three half-pence each, or sometimes a franc per dozen. Thrushes, moreover, are considered game, and occasionally the gendarmes succeed in catching a poacher, but so mixed are one's feelings in dealing with this question that it is impossible to know whether to sympathise with the unfortunate wine-grower whom the thrush robs of his two bunches of grapes per day, the poacher who is caught and heavily fined for catching it, or with the bird itself. No one who has Browning's charming lines by heart on the thrush in an "English garden in Spring," will ever quietly sit down to such a repast, and, whenever I could, I lectured the people on this slaughter of singing birds for the dinner table, I fear to no purpose. Leaving the gourmand--whose proclivities, by the way, are much encouraged throughout every stage of his journey in the Franche-Comte--let me advise the curious to study the beautiful interior of the church of St. Anatole dominating the town, also the equestrian statue of St. Maurice in the church of that name. The effect of this bit of supreme realism is almost ludicrous. The good old saint looks like some worthy countryman trotting off to market, and not at all like a holy martyr of the church.

In the Museum is seen a medallion portrait of Courbet, to which my cicerone pointed with an expression, of horror, as that of "the artist who pulled down the Vendome column."

My next stage was Arbois, a little town travellers should see on account of its charming situation in the winding valley, or "Cluse," of the Cuisance. Nothing can be prettier, or give a greater idea of prosperity, than these rich vine-yards sloping on all sides, the grapes purpling in spite of much bad weather; orchards with their ripening fruit; fields of maize, the seed now bursting the pod, and of buckwheat now in full flower, the delicate pink and white blossom of which is so poetically called by Michelet "la neige d'ete." No serenity, no grandeur here, all is verdure, dimples, smiles; abundance of rich foliage and pasture, abundance also of clear limpid water, taking every form, springs, cascades, rivulets, the little river Cuisance winding in and out amid vineyards and pastures over its rocky bed. You must follow this charming babbling river along the narrow valley to its twin sources in tangled glen and rock; the road winding between woods, vine-yards, and fantastic crags. The cluse, a narrow valley, is just paradisiacal, a bit of Eden made up of smooth pastures, rippling water, hanging woods, and golden glens, all this bright afternoon sparkling amid dew and sunshine. At one of these river sources, you see the tufa in course of formation in the river bed; in the other, the reverse process takes place, the tufa there being dissolved. Both sites are poetic and lovely in the extreme. I was sorry to hear of the devastation committed here by the oidium, or vine blight, and the dreaded phylloxera, which has already ruined thousands, causing a loss of just half the amount of the German war indemnity. This redoubtable foe is not many leagues off! Measures are taken against the phylloxera, as against an invading army, but, at present, no remedy has been discovered; and, meantime, many once rich and happy wine-growers are reduced to beggary. It was heart-breaking to gaze on the sickly appearance of the vines already attacked by the oidium, and to hear the harrowing accounts of the misery caused by an enemy more redoubtable still. Arbois, though so charming to look at, is far from being a little Eden. It is eminently a Catholic place; atheism and immorality abound; bigotry among the women, scepticism among the men, a looseness in domestic morality among all classes characterize the population, whilst we need no information on the subject of dissipation generally. The numbers of cafes and cabarets speak volumes. There is, of course, in this townling, of not six thousand souls, a theatre, which is greatly resorted to. One old church has been turned into a theatre at Arbois, and another into the Halles, a third into the Hotel-de-Ville, a desecration we Protestants can but behold with aversion. Protestantism is a young and tender plant as yet in Arbois, the church and school, or so called culte, dating from ten years back only. The congregation consists of about fifty persons, all belonging to the poorer classes, and the position of a pastor there must be a sad one. He is constantly importuned for help, which, out of his slender income, he can ill afford to bestow, and he is surrounded by spies, detractors, and adversaries on every side. That clericalism dominates here, we need not be told. The booksellers' shops are filled with tracts about the miracles of Lourdes, rosaries, and rubrics; the streets swarm with nuns, Jesuits, and Freres Ignorantins. If you ask an intelligent lad of twelve if he can read and write, he shakes his head and says no. The town itself, which might be so attractive if a little attention were paid to hygienic and sanitary matters, is neglected and dirty. The people are talkative and amiable, and are richly endowed by nature, especially in the mathematical faculty. It is said that every peasant in these parts is a born mathematician, and curiously enough the distinguished names of Arbois are those of military engineers and lawyers, notably Generals David, Delort, and Baudrand, and the celebrated jurisconsult Courvoisier. Here, as in other towns of Franche-Comte, traces of the Spanish occupation remain in the street architecture, the arcades and picture-galleries lending character. Arbois, after Salins, is like an April glimpse of sunshine following a black thunder-cloud, so contrasted is the grace of the one with the severity of the other. Tourists never come here, and in these wayside inns the master acts as waiter and porter, the mistress as cook; they give you plenty of good food, for which they hardly like to receive anything at all, talk to you as if you were an old friend during your stay, and, at your departure, are ready to embrace you out of pure cordiality.

Something must be said about the famous Arbois wine, of which Henry the Fourth of France wrote to his friend the Duke of Mayenne upon their reconciliation:--"I have some Arbois wine in my cellar, of which I send you two bottles, for I am sure you will not dislike it." These wines, both red and yellow, find their way to connoisseurs in Paris, but are chiefly grown for home-consumption. There are several kinds, and the stranger in these regions must taste both the red and the yellow of various ages and qualities to judge of their merits. I drank some of the latter thirty years old, and certainly even to one to whom the pleasures of the palate are indifferent, it tasted much as nectar might be supposed to do on Mount Olympus. The grapes are dried on straw before making this yellow wine, and the process is a very delicate and elaborate one.

How wonderful it seems to find friends and welcomes in these unfrequented regions! Up till the moment of my departure from Arbois, a little town few English travellers have even heard of, I had been engaged in earnest friendly talk with a Protestant pastor, and also with a schoolmaster and Scripture reader from the heart of the Jura; and no sooner did I arrive at Lons-le-Saunier than I found myself as much at home in two charming family circles as if I had known them all my life. Amid the first of these I was compelled to accept hospitality, and at once took my place at the hospitable family board opposite two little curly heads, boy and girl; while, an hour or two after my arrival, I was sitting in the old-fashioned artistically furnished drawing-room of a Franche-Comte Catholic family, father, mother, son and young married daughter, all welcoming me as an old friend. This was not in the cheerful little town of Lons-le-Saunier itself, but in a neighbouring village to which I drove at once, for I knew that I had been expected several days before. Fruits, liqueurs, preserves, cakes, I know not what other good things were brought out to me, and after an hour or two delightfully spent in music and conversation, I left, promising to spend a long day with my kind friends before continuing my journey. It is impossible to give any idea of Franche-Comte hospitality; you are expected to taste of everything, and your pockets are crammed with the good things you cannot eat.

I had fortunately no experience of hotels here, but a glance I got at the first in the place, when calling there for letters, was far from inspiring confidence. A detachment of troops was passing through the town, and large numbers of officers were lodged in the hotel, turning it into a scene of indescribable confusion. The food is said to be first rate, but the rooms looked dirty and uninviting, and the noise was enough to drive anyone out of his wits. How refreshing to find myself in this quiet Presbytere on the outskirts of the town, no noise except the occasional pattering of little feet and happy sound of children's voices, almost absolute quiet indeed from morning to night! My window looks upon a charming hill clothed with vine-yards, and, immediately underneath, the large straggling garden of the Presbytere. The little church adjoins the house, and the school is also under the same roof, while the schoolmaster takes his place as a guest at the family table of the pastor. All is harmony, quiet enjoyment, and peaceful domestic life.

Ah! what a different thing is the existence of a Catholic priest from that of a Protestant pastor! On the one side, we find selfishness, sensuality, and enforced isolation from the purifying influences of home and the domestic affections; a life out of harmony with the holiest instincts of human nature, and by the force of cir-cumstances, detrimental not only to the individual himself, but to society at large--on the other, a high standard of social and domestic virtue, a career of persistent self-denial, simplicity, and dignified obedience to the natural laws and exigencies of society, a life indeed edifying to all, and, by virtue of its unselfishness, uplifting to the individual. No one who knows French life intimately can fail to be struck by the comparison between the two, and painful it is to think how the one is the rule, and the other the exception, in this favoured land of France!

CHAPTER IX.
LONS-LE-SAUNIER.

Lons-le-Saunier, capital or chef-lieu of the Department of the Jura is charmingly situated amid undulating vine-covered hills, westward, stretching the vast plain of La Bresse, eastward and southward, the Jura range, dimpled heights changing the lofty mountain ranges into distance. The town known to the Romans as Ledo Salinarius and fortified under their auspices, also a fortified town in the Middle Ages, is dominated by four hills, conspicuously rising above its undulating environment, and each of these offers a superb view from the top. My first walk was to the height of Mont-ciel, Mons Coelius of the Romans, north of the town, and a delightful walk it is, leading us upward between vineyards to a broad open space planted with fine trees, and sufficiently large to afford camping ground for soldiers. From this summit we gain a wonderful prospect, vineyard, hill, and valley, with villages dotted here and there, picturesque mediaeval castles crowning many epochs, and far away the vast plain stretching from the Jura to Burgundy, and the majestic mountain ranges bounding on either side the east horizon. This walk is so easy that our little companion of four years old could make it without fatigue, and there are many others equally delightful, and not more fatiguing. We rested for awhile on the hill top eating grapes, then slowly descended, stopping on our way to enter the chapel of the Jesuits and school-buildings, both commanding a splendid site on the wooded incline. There were of course women in the confessionals, and painted images of saints and miracle-workers in abundance, before which people were kneeling with tiny images hugged to their breasts, like the pagans of old. Image worship, indeed, idolatry in the purest form, is carried on to a tremendous extent here, witness the number of images exposed for sale in the shop-windows.

But the excursion to be made from Lons-le-Saunier is that to the wonderful rock-shut valley and old Abbey of Baume, Baume-les-Messieurs, as it is called, to distinguish it from the town of Baume-les-Dames, near Besancon. This is reached by a delightful drive of an hour and a half, or easily on foot by good pedestrians, and is on no account to be omitted. We, of course, take the former course, having two little fellow-travellers, aged respectively four and two and a half years old, who, perched on our knees, are as much delighted as ourselves with the beauty of everything. We soon reach the top of the valley, a deep, narrow, rock-enclosed valley or gorge, and, leaving our carriage, prepare to descend on foot. At first sight, the zig-zag path along what appears to be the perpendicular side of these steep, lofty rocks, appears perilous, not to say impracticable, but it is neither one nor the other. This mountain stair-case, called the Echelles de Baume, may be descended in all security by sure-footed people not given to giddiness; our driver, leaving his quiet horse for a time, shoulders one child, my companion shoulders another, I followed with the basket, and in twenty minutes we are safely landed at the base of the cliffs we had just quitted, not yet quite knowing how we had got there! These rocky walls, shutting in the valley, or combe, as it is called, so closely that seldom any ray of sunshine can penetrate, are very lofty, and encircle it from end to end with majestic effect. It is, indeed, a winding little islet of green, threaded by a silvery stream, and rendered naturally impregnable by fortress-like rocks. We rest on the turf for a while, whilst the children munch their cakes and admire the noise of the mill opposite to us, and the dazzling waters of the source, pouring little cascades from the dark mountain-side into the valley. The grottoes and stalactite caverns of this combe are curious alike within and without, and in their inmost recesses is a small lake, the depth of which has never yet been sounded. Both lake and stalactite caves, however, can only be seen at certain seasons of the year, and then with difficulty.

The tiny river issuing from the cleft is called the Seille, and very lovely is the deep, narrow valley of emerald green through which it murmurs so musically. The mountain gorge opens by little and little as we proceed, showing velvety pastures where little herdsmen and herdswomen are keeping their cows; goats, black and white, browse on the steep rocks as securely as flies on a ceiling, and abundance of trees grow by the road-side. The valley winds for half a mile to the straggling village of Baume, and there the stupendous natural fortifications of cliff and rock come to an end. Nothing finer in the way of scenery is to be found throughout the Jura than this, and it is quite peculiar, being unlike any other mountain conformation I have ever seen, whilst the narrow winding valley of soft gold-green is in beautiful contrast with the rugged grandeur, not to say savageness, of its environment.

The buildings of this once important Abbey of Baume are now turned into a farm-house, but enough remains to bespeak the former magnificence of this most aristocratic monastery,[3] to which none could be admitted without furnishing proof of pure degree of nobility on both the paternal and maternal sides. Adjoining the Abbey is the Church, which possesses at least one chef-d'oeuvre in its retable.

This altar-piece of wood appears to belong to the fifteenth century, and is in the form of a triptych, the wings being enriched within and without by paintings in excellent preservation. The interior is divided into six compartments, in which are represented the various scenes of the life and passion of Christ. The various figures are finely sculptured, and covered with gold. Other paintings by the same artist decorate the walls of the Church.

One tomb, that of an abbe of Baume, is very beautiful, being ornamented with seven small statuettes of weeping monks, who occupy little gothic niches. The expression and attitude of these figures are touching in the extreme. All these monuments are highly interesting, and worthy of being studied in detail. The Church is disfigured by not a few modern frivolities and vulgarities.

Many objects illustrating the pre-historic and most ancient periods of French history have been found at Baume; bronze weapons and ornaments, Gallo-Roman relics, tombs, statuettes, &c., whilst a Roman camp, the largest in the Jura, has been traced on the summit of the rocks. This was destined to protect the road from Lyons to the Rhine, and occupied the height known as Mount Sermus.

Baume shared the fate of most other ecclesiastical establishments in the icono-clastic period of the French Revolution, and when we consider what the pitch of popular fury was then, we are rather tempted to wonder that anything was left, rather than that so many treasures were destroyed.

Our way home lay through the picturesque valley of the Seille, and past many places celebrated for their wines or antiquities. Vines, maize, buckwheat, potatoes, and hay covered the hillside and the plain, whilst poplar and fruit trees gave abun-

---

3   Consult Roussel's "Dictionnaire de Franche-Comte" on the subject. It is very voluminous, but like any other work on Franche-Comte, may be consulted in the public library of Lons-le-Saunier without trouble or formality.

dant shadow. We pass Voiteur, with its ruins; Chateau Chalon, ancient Celtic oppidum, renowned for its wines, like Tokay, 'veritable Madere sec Francais, genereux,'
the Chateau du Pin, massive donjon perched on a hill, and still habitable, where
Henry IV. sojourned, and other picturesque and interesting sites, reaching home
before dusk. In fine weather the inhabitants of Lons-le-Saunier frequently make
pic-nic parties to Baume, breakfasting in the valley, but, alas! fine pic-nic weather is
as rare in Franche-Comte as in England this year, and autumn, always sets in early;
already the mornings and evenings are really cold, and a fire would be a luxury. We
do, however, get a fine day now and then, with a few hours of warm sunshine, and I
had one of these for a visit to my friends living in the neighbourhood, whom I have
before mentioned.

This little village in question is captivatingly situated at the foot of the first Jura
range, about a mile from Lons-le-Saunier. As I have before said, throughout this entire journey, whenever I have spoken of a mountain it must be understood to mean
a mountain of the Jura chain, which begins here, and only ends at Belfort, where
you enter the region of the Vosges, and all along consists of the same limestone formation, only here and there a vein of granite being found. My friend's house is delightful, standing in the midst of orchards, gardens, and vines, the fine rugged peak
called Mont d'Orient--of which he is the owner--rising above. On a glorious day
like this, we, of course, all set off for the mountain-top, and a wonderfully beautiful
climb it was, amid vineyards, pastures, and groves of walnut trees. The grapes here
are, alas! attacked in many places by the blight oidium, and this year the season has
been so wet and cold, that as they must be gathered after the first white frost, they
have no chance of ripening. As a natural result, the year's wine will be sour, and
sold at a considerable loss to the growers. We stopped on our way to taste the grapes
here and there, but as yet none are ripe, though we are in the last days of September. After steadily climbing for an hour, we reached the mountain-top, and sat
down to enjoy the view, having in sight on one side the immense plain stretching
from the Jura to the hills of the Cote d'Or, on the other, in very clear weather, the
Jura range and the top of Mont Blanc. Never shall I forget this charming walk with
my host, his son, and daughter, all three able to give me any information I was in
need of concerning their beloved Franche-Comte. As we returned home by another
way through lovely little woods, dells, and glades, we encountered more than one

sportsman in blue blouse, who got into the covert of the wood as fast as he could, in quest of thrushes. "A poacher," my host said, shrugging his shoulders. "Mais que voulez-vous; il y en a tant." Poaching is carried on so largely that very little game is to be had; the severe penalties inflicted by the law having little deterrent effect.

My host told me much of interest concerning the peasants and their ways. The land here belongs to the people, but the rural population is not wealthy, as in Seine et Marne and other regions. The bad vine seasons often ruin the farmer, and much improvidence prevails. In many places the proprietor of a vineyard hires small patches of land to cultivate, but that avidity in making purchases found elsewhere does not exist here. Land is cheap, but labour very dear, and the peasant therefore mistrusts such investments of capital, if he possesses any; and the liability to the failure in the vine crops necessarily checks enterprise in that direction.

On our return, we found an excellent gouter, as these afternoon collations are called, substitutes, in fact, for our four o'clock tea. We drank each other's health after the old fashion with the celebrated Arbois wine, called le vin de Paille, from the process the grape goes through, being dried in straw before fermentation. This vin de Paille has an exquisite flavour and is very costly and rare, even in these parts, being chiefly grown by amateurs for themselves. It is clear as crystal, and yellow as gold. Sorry indeed was I to quit these kind and charming friends with whom I would gladly have spent many a day. They had so much to show me--antique furniture, a collection of old French faience, sketches in oils, the work of my host himself, books on the history of Franche-Comte, collections, geological and archaeological, bearing on the history of the country; last, but not least, my hostess--admirable type of the well-bred Catholic chatelaine of former days--was an accomplished musician, ready to delight her guest with selections from Chopin and Schubert, and other favorite composers. But, however reluctantly on both sides, our adieux had to be made, a promise being exacted from me to visit Franche-Comte ere long again.

I shall carry away no more agreeable recollection of Eastern France than this pleasant country home and its occupants in the Jura, father, mother, young son and daughter, all vying with each other in making my visit pleasant and profitable. It is touching to be so welcomed, so taken leave of in the midst of a remote foreign place, all the more so when there was no Protestantism and Republicanism, only natural liking and a community of tastes, to bring us together! French Protestants welcome us English folks--presumably Protestants too--as their kindred, but let it not be supposed that even in the heart of Catholic regions like this, we are now generally regarded with abhorrence as aliens from the true faith--culture, high tastes, and tolerance naturally go hand in hand.

In order to get a good idea of the scenery here the plain must be visited as well as the mountains, and very beautiful it is as seen from such eminences as those occupied by the Chateaux de l'Etoile and Arlay; both excursions to be accomplished in a long afternoon, even with a halt for gouter at the former place, its owners being friends of my host and hostess. This modern chateau occupies the site of the old, and commands wide views on every side, in the far distance the valley of the Saone and the mountains of the Cote d'Or, with the varied, richly wooded plain at our feet. The Bresse, as this is called, is not healthy for the most part, and the population suffer from marsh fever, but it is well cultivated and very productive; vines grow sparsely in the plain, the chief crops consisting of corn, maize, beetroot, hemp, &c. A curious feature of farming in the Bresse is the number of artificial ponds which are seen in different directions. These ponds are allowed to remain for four years, and are then filled up, producing very rich crops. In the meantime a good deal of fish is thus procured. The land is parcelled out into small farms, the property of small peasant proprietors, as in the vineyard regions of the Jura. After having admired one prospect after another, hill and valley, wood and pine forest, far off mountain ranges and wide purple plain, we were of course not permitted to go away without tasting the famous wine for which the Etoile is celebrated, and other good things. Useless it is to protest upon these occasions, not only once, but twice and even thrice you are compelled, in spite of remonstrances, to partake, and glasses are touched after the old fashion. We then quitted our kind host and hostess of this airy perch, and continued our journey, still in the Plains, to Arlay, a village. dominated by the majestic ruins of an old feudal castle, standing in the midst of fine old trees worthy of an English park.

Arlay was built in the ninth century by Gerard de Boussillon, and now belongs to the Prince d'Aremberg whose handsome modern chateau lies at its foot. The Prince of Aremberg is one of the largest landowners in France, and we were told had not visited this splendid possession for ten years.

Many other no less interesting excursions are to be made from Lons-le-Saunier, but I am a belated traveller, overtaken by autumn rains and chills, and must hasten on my way. September and October are often glorious months in the Jura, but it is safest to come sooner, and then picnics innumerable can be made, and fine weather relied upon from day to day. The town itself is cheerful, but offers little of interest to the tourist, beyond the salines, or salt-works, which, however, are on a much smaller scale than at Salins, and one or two other objects of interest. A curious feature in its architecture are the arcades in the streets, similar to those at Arbois, and some other old towns in Franche-Comte, relics of the Spanish occupation. There is also an unmistakeable Spanish element to be found in the population, witness the black eyes, and hair, and dark rich complexions of a type common enough here, yet quite distinct from that of the true French stock. The people as a rule are well-made, stalwart, and good-looking, polite to strangers, and very voluble in conversation.

If the antiquities of Lons-le-Saunier are insignificant, no one can fail, however, to be struck with the handsome public buildings, chiefly modern, which are on a scale quite magnificent for a town of only eleven thousand inhabitants. The hospital, the caserne, or barracks, the lycee, the ecole normale, the bank, all these are large enough and magnificent enough, one would suppose, for any but the largest provincial towns; the streets are spacious, and the so-called Grande Place, in the centre of the town, is adorned by a fine statue of General Lecourbe, where formerly stood a statue of Pichegru; this was presented by Charles X. to the municipality in 1826, and broken by the townspeople in 1830. The gardens of the hospital are adorned by a bust of the great anatomist, Bichat, whose birth-place, like that of Homer, is disputed. Bourg-en-Bresse disputes the honour with Lons-le-Saunier, and Bourg possesses the splendid monument to Bichat's memory by David d'Angers. The museum is worth visiting, less for the sake of its archaeological collection than its sculptural gallery, chiefly consisting of works by a contemporary native artist, Perrault.

One of the prettiest strolls in the neighbourhood of this most "spazierlich" town, as the Germans say, i.e., a town to be enjoyed by pedestrians, is the old little village of Montaigu, which is reached after half an hour's climb among the vineyards. As we mount, we get a magnificent panorama to our right, the plain of La Bresse, to-day blue and dim as a summer sea; to our left, the Jura range, dark purple shadows here and there flecking the green mountain sides; the pretty little town of Lons-le-Saunier at our feet. On this bright September day everything is glowing and beautiful; the air is fresh and invigorating, and the sun still hot enough to ripen the grapes which we see on every side.

Montaigu, however, is not visited for the sake of these lovely prospects so much as its celebrity as a birth-place. This little hamlet and former fortress, perched on a mountain top, is, perhaps, little changed in outward appearance since a soldier-poet, destined to revolutionise France with a song, was born there a hundred years ago. The immortal, inimitable Marseillaise, which electrified every French man, woman, or child then, and stirs the calmest with profound emotion now, is, indeed, the Revolution incorporated into poetry, and the words and music of the young soldier, Rouget de Lisle, have played a more important part in history than any other in any age or nation. Alas! the Marseillaise has been sadly misappropriated since, and cannot be heard by those who know French history without pain; yet it has played a glorious part, and, doubtless, contributed to many a victory when France saw itself beset with enemies on every side in its first and greatest struggle for liberty. It is not to be expected in a country so priest-ridden as this, that a statue to Rouget de Lisle should be erected in his native town; but surely an inscription, merely stating the fact, might be placed on the house wherein he first saw the light. There is nothing to distinguish it from any other, except a solid iron gateway through which we looked into a little court-yard, and upon a modest yet well-to-do bourgeois dwelling of the olden time.

The entire village street has an antiquated look, and the red roof tops, with corner pieces for letting off the snow, which falls abundantly here, are picturesque, if not suggestive of comfort. On our way back to the town, we found all the beauty and fashion of Lons-le-Saunier collected on the promenade of La Chevalerie to hear the military band, which, as usual in French towns, plays on Sunday afternoons. This same promenade is famous in history, for here it was, on the 31st May, 1815, that Marshal Ney, having decided upon going over to the army of the Emperor Napoleon, summoned his troops, and issued the famous proclamation beginning with the words: "La cause des Bourbons est a jamais perdue." Ney deceived himself, as well as the Royalists, and was shot soon after the final overthrow at Waterloo. There is no lack of pleasant walks inside the town as well as in the environs, whilst, perhaps, no other of its size possesses so many cafes and cabarets. In fact, Lons-le-Saunier is a place where amusement is the order of the day, and, of course, possesses its theatre, museum, and public library; the first, perhaps, being much more popular than the two latter. "Eat, drink, and be merry, for to-morrow you die," is the maxim of the light-hearted, we must even say frivolous population. While the men amuse themselves in the cafes, the women go to the confessional, and no matter at what hour you enter a church, you are sure to find them thus occupied. The Jesuits have established a large training-school here, une maison de noviciat, so called; and conventual institutions abound, as at Arbois. Just beyond the pleasant garden of the Presbytere is a large building of cloistered nuns, wretched women, belonging to the upper ranks of society, who have shut themselves up to mortify the flesh and practise all kinds of puerilities for the glory of the church. All the handsome municipal institutions, large hospitals, orphanages, asylums for the aged, &c., are in the hands of the nuns and priests, and woe betide the unfortunate Protestant who is driven to seek such shelter!

The same battle occurs here over Protestant interments as in other parts of Franche-Comte. In some cases it is necessary for the prefets to send gendarmes, and have the law carried out by force; the village mayors being generally uneducated men, mere tools of the cures.

After the idyllic pictures I have drawn of other parts of France, I am reluctantly obliged to draw a very different picture of society here. The army and the celibate clergy, the soldier and the priest--such are the demoralizing elements that undermine domestic morality and family life in garrison, priest-ridden towns like this. Drink and debauchery fill the prisons, and the taint of immorality is not limited to one class alone. How can it be otherwise? seeing that while the heads of families openly profess unbelief, and deride their priests, they permit their wives and daughters to go to confession, and confide their children to the spiritual teachers they profess to abhor? This point was clearly brought out by the Pere Hyacinthe in one of his recent discourses in Paris, and his words struck home. Next to the celibate priesthood, it is the army that brings about such a state of things. Householders in Lons-le-Saunier will tell you that, no matter whether their female servants be young, middle-aged, or old, they have to bar and bolt their doors at night as if against marauding Arabs in remote settlements of Algeria. Even when these precautions are taken, the sound of whistling outside the kitchen door at nightfall will often indicate the presence of loafers on their evil quest. In the rural districts domestic morality is at a very low ebb also, and on the whole there is much to be done here by both reformer and educationalist.

I left Lons-le-Saunier early on a bright September morning, the children being lifted, still drowsy, out of their little beds to bid their English friend good-bye. Several diligences start simultaneously from the Bureau des Messageries here for different places in the heart of the Jura, so that tourists cannot do better than make this a starting place. No matter what direction they take, they will find themselves landed in the midst of glorious mountain scenery, and romantic little towns and valleys, unknown to the majority of the travelling world. This is the charm of travelling in these parts. The tourist is breaking virgin soil wherever he goes, and if he has to rough it at every stage, at least he receives substantial reward. My route, marked out for me beforehand by experienced Jurassiens, lay by way of Champagnole and Morez to St. Claude, the ancient little bishopric in the heart of the Jura highlands, thence to Nantua, thus zig-zagging right through the country.

CHAPTER X.
CHAMPAGNOLE AND MOREZ.

On quitting Lons-le-Saunier for Champagnole, our way led through rich tracts of vineyard; but no sooner were we fairly among the mountains than the vine disappeared altogether, and scant culture and pastures took its place. We also soon perceive the peculiar characteristics of the Jura range, which so essentially distinguish it from the Alps. These mountains do not take abrupt shapes of cones and sugar-loaves, but stretch out in vast sweeps with broad summits and lateral ridges, features readily seized, and lending to the landscape its most salient characteristics. Not only are we entering the region of lofty mountains and deep valleys, but of numerous industrial centres, also the land of mediaeval warfare and legend, whence arose the popular saying:

"Comtois, rends-toi,   Nenni, ma foi."

Our journey, of four hours, takes us through a succession of grandiose and charming prospects, and lonely little villages, at which we pick up letters, and drop numbers of Le Petit Journal, probably all the literature they get. Gorge, crag, lake and ravine, valley, river, and cascade, pine forests crowning sombre ridges, broad hill-sides alive with the tinkling of cattle bells, pastoral scenes separating frowning peaks, all these we have to rejoice the eye and much more. The beautiful Lake of Challin, we only see in the distance, though most enticingly inviting nearer inspection, and all this valley of the Ain might, indeed, detain the tourist several days. The river Ain has its source near Champagnole, and flows through a broad beautiful valley southwards, but the only way to get an idea of the geography of the place is to climb a mountain, maps avail little.

On alighting at the Hotel Dumont, the sight of an elegant landlady, in spotless white morning gown, was re-assuring, and when I was conducted to a bedroom with bells, clean floors, proper washing apparatus, and other comforts, my heart quite leapt. There is nothing to see at Champagnole but the saw-mills, the "click, click" of which you hear at every turn. Saw-making by machinery is the principal industry here, and is worth inspecting. But if the town itself is uninteresting, it offers a variety of delicious walks and drives, and must be a very healthy summer resort, being five hundred yards above the level of the plain. I went a little way on the road to Les Planches, and nothing could be more solemnly beautiful than the black pines pricking against the deep blue sky, and the golden light playing on the ferns and pine-stems below; before us, a vista of deep gorge and purple mountain chain, on either side the solemn serried lines of the forest. The good pedestrian should follow this road to Les Planches, as splendid a walk as any in the Jura. No less delightful, though in a different way, is the winding walk by the river. The Ain here rushes past with a torrent like thunder, and rolls and tosses over a stony bed, having on either side green slopes and shady ways. Those travellers, like myself, contented with a bit of modest mountaineering, will delight in the three hours' climb of Mount Rivol, a broad pyramidal mountain, eight hundred yards in height, dominating the town. A very beautiful walk is this for fairly good walkers, and though the sun is intense, the air is sharp and penetrating. On our way, we find plenty of ripe wild mulberries with which to refresh ourselves, and abundance of the blue-fringed gentian to delight our eyes.

So steep are these mountain sides, that it is like scaling a wall, but after an hour and a half we are rewarded by finding ourselves on the top; a broad plateau covering many acres richly cultivated, with farm-buildings in the centre. Here we enjoy one of those magnificent panoramas so plentiful in the Jura, and which must be seen to be realized. On one side we have the verdant valley of the Ain, the river flowing gently through green fields and softly dimpled hills; on another, Andelot with its bridge and the lofty rocks bristling round Salins; on the third side, the road leading to Pontarlier amid pine-forest and limestone crags, and above this, a sight more majestic still, namely, the vast parallel ranges of the Jura, deepest purple, crested in the far away distance with a silvery peak whose name takes our very breath away. We are gazing on Mont Blanc! a sight as grandiose and inspiring as the distant glimpse of the Pyramids from Cairo! We would fain have lingered long before this glorious picture, but the air was too cold to admit of a halt after our heating walk in the blazing sun. The great drawback to travelling in the Jura, indeed, is this terrible fickleness of climate. As a rule, even thus early in the autumn, you are obliged to make several toilettes a day, putting on winter clothes when you get up, and towards mid-day exchanging them for the lightest summer attire till sunset, when again you need the warmest clothing. Winter sets in very early here, there is no spring, properly speaking; five months of fine warm weather have to be set against seven of frost and snow; yet in spite of the bitterness and long duration of these winters, little or no provision seems to be made against the cold. There are no carpets, curtains, and generally no fire-places in the bedrooms, all is cold, cool, and bare as in Egypt, and many are approached from without. The people must enjoy a wonderful vigour of health and robustness of constitution, or they could not resist such hardships as these, and what a Jura winter is, makes one shudder to think of. Snow lies often twelve feet deep on the road, and journeys are performed by sledges, as in Russia.

I took the diligence from Champagnole to Morez, and it is as yet the only ill-advised thing I have done on this journey. The fact is, and intending travellers should note it, that there are only three modes of travelling in these parts, firstly, by hiring a private carriage and telegraphing for relays; secondly, by accomplishing short stages on foot, by far the most agreeable method for hardy pedestrians, or thirdly, to give up the most interesting spots altogether. The diligence must not be taken into account as a means of locomotion at all, for as there is no competition, and French people are much too amiable or indifferent to make complaints, the truth must be told, that the so-called Messageries du Jura are about as badly managed as can possibly be. Unfortunate travellers are not only so cramped that they arrive at their destination more dead than alive, but even in the coupe they see nothing of the country. Thus the glorious bit of country we passed through from Champagnole to Morez was entirely lost on me, simply because the diligence is not a public conveyance, but an instrument of torture. The so-called coupe was so small, warm and low, that the three unfortunate occupants of it, a stout gentleman, a nun, and myself, were so closely wedged in that we could not stir a limb, whilst the narrow slice of landscape before us was hidden by the driver and two other passengers, all three of whom smoked incessantly. There were several equally unfortunate travellers packed in the body of the carriage, and others outside on the top of the luggage, all arriving at their destination feeling much as if they had been subjected to the bastinado! Nothing could be worse, and whilst the heat was intense for the first part of the journey, the latter part was bitterly cold, yet it was impossible to move one's arm in order to draw on a wrap. Cold, heat, cramp, and dejection are the portion of those who trust themselves to the accursed Messageries du Jura.

My sufferings were alleviated by the nun, who managed to extract some fruit from her basket and handed me a pear and a peach. I had said so many hard things about nuns during my life, that I hesitated, but the fleshly temptation was too strong, and I greedily accepted the drop of water held out in the desert. To my great relief afterwards, I found that my companion was not occupied in cooking up theology for the detriment of others, but in the far more innocent task of making soups and sauces. In fact, she was cook to the establishment to which she belonged, and a very homely, excellent soul she seemed. She turned from her pears and peaches to her prayer-book and rosary with equal delectation. It was harrowing to think that during these five hours we were passing through some of the most romantic scenery of the Jura, yet all we could do, by occasionally stretching out our necks, was to get a glance at the lovely lakes, pine-topped heights, deep gorges, gigantic cliffs towering to the sky, adorable little cascades springing from silvery mountain-sides, gold-green table-lands lying between hoary peaks; everything delightful was there, could we but see! Meantime, we had been climbing ever since we quitted Champagnole, and at one point marked by a stone, were a thousand yards above the sea-level. The little villages perched on the mountain-tops that we were passing through, are all seats of industry; clock manufactories, fromageries, or cheese-farms on a large scale, and so on.

The population indeed depends, not upon agriculture, but upon industries for support, and many of the wares fabricated in these isolated Jura villages find their way all over the world. From St. Laurent, where we stopped to change horses, the traveller who is indifferent to cramps, bruises and contortions, may exchange diligences, and instead of taking the shorter and straighter road to St. Claude, may follow the more picturesque route by way of the wonderful little lake of Grandvaux, shut in by mountains, and peopled with fish of all kinds, water-hens, and other wild birds. We are now in the wildest and most grandiose region of the Jura, and whichever road we take is sure to lead us through grand scenery. But much as I had heard of the savage beauty of Grandvaux, further subjection to the torture we were thus enduring was not to be thought of, so we went straight on to Morez, after the tremendous ascent I have just described, our road curving quickly downwards, and coming all at once on the long straggling little town, framed in by lofty mountains on every side.

Next morning was Sunday, and I went in search of the Protestant school-house, where I knew a kind welcome awaited me. I was delighted to find a new handsome building, standing conspicuously in a pleasant garden, over the doors, engraved in large letters, "Culte et Ecole Evangelique." The sound of childrens' voices told me that some kind of lesson or prayer was going on, so I waited in the garden till the doors opened and a dozen neatly dressed boys and girls poured out. Then I went in, and found the wife of the schoolmaster and scripture-reader, a sweet young woman, who, in her husband's absence, had been holding a Bible class. She showed me over the place, and an exquisitely clean quiet little room she had prepared for me, but as I had arrived rather late on the night before, I had taken a room at the hotel, which was neither noisy nor uncomfortable. We spent the afternoon together, and as we walked along the beautiful mountain road that superb September Sunday, many interesting things she told me of her husband's labours in their isolated mountain home. Protestantism is indeed here a tender plant, exposed to the cold blast of adverse winds, but if it takes healthy root, well will it be for the social, moral, and intellectual advancement of the people. We must never lose sight of the fact that, putting theology out of the question, Protestantism means morality, hygiene, instruction, and above all, a high standard of truth and family life; and on these grounds, if on no other, all really concerned in the future and well-being of France must wish it God-speed.

This is not the place for a comparison between Protestantism and Catholicism, even as social influences, but one thing I must insist upon, namely, that it is only necessary to live among French Protestants and compare what we find there with what we find among their Catholic neighbours, to feel how uncompromisingly the first are the promoters of progress, and the latter its adversaries.

The position of Morez is heavenly beautiful, but the town itself hideous. Nature having put the finishing touch to her choice handiwork, man has come in to mar and spoil the whole. The mountains, clothed with brightest green, rise grandly towards the sky, but all along the narrow gorge of the Bienne, in which Morez lies, stand closely compacted masses of many storied manufactories and congeries of dark, unattractive houses. There is hardly a garden, a chalet, or villa to redeem the prevailing, crushing ugliness; yet, for all that, if you can once get over the profound sadness induced by this strange contrast, nothing can be more delightful and exhilarating than the mountain environment of this little seat of industry. Morez, indeed, is a black diamond set in richest gold. The place abounds in cafes, and on this Sunday afternoon, when all the manufactories are closed, the cafes are full to overflowing, and on the lovely suburban road, winding above the mountains, we meet few working-men with their families enjoying a walk. The cabaret absorbs them all.

The working hours here are terribly long; from five o'clock in the morning till seven at night, the bulk of the population are at their posts, men, women, and young people--children, I was going to say--but fortunately public opinion is stepping in to prevent the abuse of juvenile labour so prevalent, and good laws on the subject will, it is hoped, ere long be enacted. The wages are low, three or four francs a-day being the maximum, and as the cost of living is high here, it is only by the conjoint labours of all the members of a household that it can be kept together. Squalor and unthrift abound, and there are no founders of cites ouvrieres to make the workman's home what it should be. He is badly housed as well as being badly paid, and no wonder that the cafe and the cabaret are seized upon as the only recreations for what leisure he gets. It is quite worth while--for those travellers who ever stay a whole week anywhere--to stay a week here in order to see the curious industries which feed the entire population of the town and neighbouring villages, and are known all over the commercial world. The chief objects of manufacture are spectacle-glasses, spits, clocks, nails, electro-plate, drawn-wire, shop-plates in iron and enamel, files, and dish-covers; but of these the three first are by far the most important. Several hundred thousand spectacle glasses and clocks, and sixty thousand spits, are fabricated here yearly, and all three branches of industry afford curious matter for inquiry. Thus the first of spectacle-making, or lunetterie, resolves itself into a scientific study of noses! it will easily be seen that the manufacturer of spectacles on a grand scale must take into account the physiognomies of the different nations which import his wares. A long-nosed people will require one shaped pair of spectacles, an aquilline-nosed another, a nez retrousse a third; and accordingly we find that spectacles nicely adjusted to such peculiarities are fabricated, one kind supplying the American, a second the Spanish, a third the English market, and so on. So wonderfully quick is the process that a pair of spectacles can be made for three-halfpence! The clocks made by machinery at Morez are chiefly of the cheap kind, but wear well, and are to be found in almost every cottage in France. The prices vary from ten to twenty francs, and are thus within reach of the poorest. A more expensive kind are found in churches, public offices, schools, railway-stations, and manufactories, not only in France, but in remote quarters of the world. Spain largely imports these elegant inexpensive clocks fabricated in the heart of the Jura, and they find their way to China! Each separate part has its separate workshop, and the whole is a marvellous exhibition of dexterity, quickness, and apt division of labour.

A large manufactory of electrotype plate, modelled on those of England, notably the Elkington ware, has been founded here within recent years, and is very flourishing, exporting on a vast scale to remote countries. There is a manufactory of electric clocks, also of recent date. All day long, therefore, the solemn silence of these mountains is broken by the noise of mill-wheels and rushing waters, and if it is the manufactories that feed the people, it is the rivers that feed the manufactories. The Jura, indeed, may be said to depend on its running streams and rivers for its wealth, each and all a Pactolus in its way, flowing over sands of gold. Nowhere has water power been turned to better account than at Morez, where a very Ariel, it is forced by that all-omnipotent Prospero man, the machine-maker, to do his behests, here turning a wheel, there flowing into the channels prepared for it, and on every side dispensing riches and civilization.

Delightful and refreshing it is to get beyond reach of these never-resting mill-wheels, and follow the mountain-torrent and the rushing streams to their home, where they are at liberty and untamed. Innumerable delicious haunts are to be found in the neighbourhood of Morez, also exhilarating panoramas of the Jura and Switzerland from the mountain-tops. There is nothing to be called agriculture, for in our gradual ascent we have alternately left behind us the vine, corn, maize, walnuts and other fruit trees, reaching the zone of the gentian, the box-tree, the larch, and the pine. These apparently arid limestone slopes and summits, however, have velvety patches here and there, and such scattered pastures are a source of almost incredible wealth. The famous Jura cheese, Gruyere so called, is made in the isolated chalets perched on the crest of a ravine, and nestled in the heart of a valley, which for the seven winter months are abandoned, and throughout the other five swarm like bee-hives with industrious workers. As soon as the snow melts, the peasants return to the mountains, but in winter all is silent, solitary, and enveloped in an impenetrable veil of snow. The very high-roads are imperceptible then, and the village sacristan rings the church bells in order to guide the belated traveller to his home.

My friend, the schoolmaster's wife, found me agreeable travelling companions for the three hours' drive to St. Claude, which we made in a private carriage, in order to see the country. Very nice people they were, Catholics belonging to the petite bourgeoisie, and much useful information they gave me about things and people in their native province. The weather is perfect, with a warm south wind, a bright blue sky, and feathery clouds subduing the dazzling heavens. We get a good notion of the Jura in its sterner and more arid aspect during this zig-zag drive, first mounting, then descending. Far away, the brown bare mountain ridges rise against the clear heavens, whilst just below we see steep wooded crags dipping into a gorge where the little river Bienne curls on its impetuous way. There are no less than three parallel roads at different levels from Morez to St. Claude, and curious it was from our airy height--we had chosen the highest--to survey the others, the one cut along the mountain flank midway, the other winding deep down close to the river-side. These splendid roads are kept in order by the Communes, which are often rich in this Department, possessing large tracts of forest. I never anywhere saw roads so magnificently kept, and, of course, this acids greatly to the comfort of travellers. Were the roads bad, indeed, what would become of them?

After climbing for an hour we suddenly begin to descend, our road sweeping round the mountain sides with tremendous curves for about two hours or more, when all of a sudden we seemed to swoop down upon St. Claude, the little bishopric in the heart of the mountains. The effect was magical. We appeared to have been plunged from the top of the world to the bottom! In fact, you go up and down such tremendous heights in the Jura that I should think it must be much like travelling in a balloon.

CHAPTER XI.
ST. CLAUDE: THE BISHOPRIC
IN THE MOUNTAINS.

I was prepared to be fascinated with St. Claude, to find it wholly unique and bewitching, to greet it with enthusiasm, and bid it farewell with regret. It has been described so glowingly by different writers--alike its history, site, and natural features are so curious and poetic, such a flavour of antiquity clings to it, that perhaps no other town in the Jura is approached with equal expectation. Nor can any preconceived notion of the attractiveness of St. Claude, however high, be disappointed, if visited in fine weather. It is really a marvellous place, and takes the strangest hold on the imagination. The antique city, so superbly encased with lofty mountains, is as proud as it is singular, depending on its own resources, and not putting on a smile to attract the stranger. Were a magician to sweep away these humming wheels, hammering mill-stones, gloomy warehouses, and put smiling pleasure-grounds and coquettish villas in their place, St. Claude might become as fashionable a resort as the most favourite Swiss or Italian haunts. But in its present condition it does not lay itself out to please, and the town is built in the only way building was possible, up and down, on the edge of the cliffs here, in the depths of a hollow there, zig-zag, just anyhow. High mountains hem it round, and two rivers run in their deep beds alongside the irregular streets, a superb suspension bridge spanning the Valley of the Tacon, a depth of fifty yards. Higher up, a handsome viaduct spans the Valley of La Bienne, on either side of these two stretch clusters of houses, some sloping one way, some another, with picturesque effect. To find your way in these labyrinthine streets, alleys, and terraces is no easy matter, whilst at every turn you come upon the sound of wheels, betokening some manufactory of the well-known, widely imported St. Claude ware, consisting chiefly of turnery, carved and inlaid toys, and fancy articles in wood, bone, ivory, stag's horn, &c. Small hanging gardens are seen wherever a bit of soil is to be had, whilst the town also possesses a fine avenue of old trees turned into a public promenade. St. Claude is really wonderful, and the more you see of it the more you are fascinated. Though far from possessing the variety of artistic fountains of Salins, several here are very pretty and ornamental--notably one surrounded with the most captivating little Loves in bronze, riding dolphins. The sight and sound of rippling water every-where are delicious; rivers and fountains, fountains and rivers, everywhere! whilst the summer-like heat of mid-day makes both all the more refreshing. St. Claude has everything--the frowning mountain-crests of Salins, the pine-clad fastnesses of Champagnole, the romantic mountain walls of Morez, sublimity, grace, pictur-esqueness, grandeur, all are here, and all at this season of the year embellished by the crimson and amber tints of autumn.

What lovely things did I see during an hour and a half's walk to the so-called Pont du Diable! Taking one winding mountain road of many, and following the clear winding deep green river, though high above it, I came to a scene as wild, beautiful, and solitary as the mind can picture, above bare grey cliffs, lower down fairy-like little lawns of brightest green, deeper down still, the river making a dozen cascades over its stony bed, and round about the glorious autumn foliage, under a cloudless sky. All the way I had heard, mingled with the roar of the impetuous river, the sound of mill-wheels, and I passed I know not how many manufactories, most of which lie so deep down in the heart of the gorges that they do not spoil the scenery. The ugly blot is hidden, or at least inconspicuous. As I turn back, I have on one side a vast velvety slope, sweeping from mountain to river, terrace upon terrace of golden-green pasture, where a dozen little girls are keeping their kine; on the other steep limestone precipices, all a tangle of brushwood, with only here and there a bit of scant pasturage. The air is transparent and reviving, a south wind caresses us as we go, nothing can be more heavenly beautiful. The blue gentian grows everywhere, and, as I pursue my way, the peasant-folks I meet with pause to say good-day and stare. They evidently find in me an outlandish look, and are quite unaccustomed to the sight of strangers.

I had pleasant acquaintances provided for me here by my friend, the schoolmaster's wife at Morez, and a very agreeable glimpse I thus obtained of French middle-class life; Catholic life, moreover, but free alike from bigotry and intolerance. Very light-hearted, lively, and well-informed were these companions of my walks at St. Claude, among them a government official, his young wife, sister, and another relation, who delighted in showing me everything. We set off one lovely afternoon for what turned out to be a four hours' walk, but not a moment too long, seeing the splendour of weather and scenery, and the amiability of my companions. We took a road that led from the back of the Cathedral by the Valley of the Tacon, a little river that has its rise in the mountain near, and falls into the Flumen close by. It is necessary to take this walk to the falls of the Flumen in order to realize fully the wonderful site of St. Claude, and the amazing variety of the surrounding scenery. Every turn we take of the upward curling road gives us a new and more beautiful picture. The valley grows deeper and deeper, the mountains on either side higher and higher, little chalets peeping amid the grey and the green, here perched on an apparently unapproachable mountain-top, there in the inmost recess of some rocky dell. As we get near the falls, we are reaching one of the most romantic points of view in all the Jura, and one of the most striking I have ever seen, so imposingly do the mountains close around us as we enter the gorge, so lovely the scene shut in by the impenetrable natural wall; for within the framework of rock, peak, and precipice are little farms, gardens, and orchards--gems of dazzling green bathed in ripest sunshine, pine-forests frowning close above these islets of luxuriance and cultivation, dells, glades, and open, lawny spaces between the ramparts of fantastically formed crags and solitary peaks, a scene recalling Kabylia, in the Atlas mountains, but unlike anything except itself. All was still, except for the roar of the tiny river and the occasional sound of timber sliding from some mountain slope into the valley below. The timber is thus transported in these parts, the woodman cutting the planks on some convenient ledge of rock, then letting it find its way to the bottom as best it can. All day long you see the trunk-cutters at work on their airy perches, now bright stairs of gold-green turf, soon to be enveloped in impenetrable masses of snow, and hear the falling planks. As we climb, we are overtaken by two timber carts, and the drivers, peasant-folks from the mountains, are old acquaintances of my companions, and suggest that the ladies should mount. We gladly do so, to the great satisfaction of the peasants, who on no account would themselves add to their horses' burden. It would have been an affront to offer these good people anything in return for their kindness. They were delighted to chat behind with Monsieur, whilst their horses, sure-footed as mules, made their way beside the winding precipice. These peasants had intelligent, good countenances, and were excellent types of the Jura mountaineer.

Having passed a tunnel cut through the rock, we soon reached the head of the valley, the end of the world, as it seems, so high, massive, and deep is the formidable mountain wall hemming it in, from whose sides the little river Tacon takes a tremendous leap into the green valley below; and not one leap, but a dozen, the several cascades uniting in a stream that meanders towards St. Claude. Before us, high above the falls, seeming to hang on a perpendicular chain of rocks, is a cluster of saw-mills. It is not more the variety of form in this scene here than the variety of colour and tone that makes it so wonderful. Everywhere the eye rests on some different outline, colour, or combination.

Would that space permitted of a detailed account here of all else that I saw in this ancient little bishopric in the mountains! St. Claude, indeed, deserves a chapter, nay, a small volume to itself; there is its history to begin with, which dates from the earliest Christian epoch in France; then its industries, each so curious in its details; lastly, the marvellous natural features of its position, a wholly unique little city is this, compared by Lamartine to Zarcle in the forests of Lebanon, and described by other Franche-Comte writers in equally glowing terms. The famous Abbey of St. Claude was visited by Louis XI in order to fulfil a vow still mysterious in history. This was under the regime of its eighty-sixth Abbot, Peter Morel, but, after a period of almost unequalled glory and magnificence, fire, pillage, and other misfortunes visited it from time to time, till the suppression of the Abbey in 1798. I went into the Cathedral with two charming young married ladies, whose acquaintance I had made during my stay, and, leaving them devoutly on their knees, inspected the beautiful and quaint stalls in carved wood of the choir; these are worth a day's study, and unfortunately are not to be had in photography, for some reason or other no photographs being permitted. Here the spirit of the Renaissance has had full play, and you find comedy mixed with pathos, practical good sense with Biblical solemnity, quaintness, beauty, grace, drollery, all in one. The middle statues in bold relief are those of the early Kings of France and the Abbots of St. Claude, besides many noteworthy saints and martyrs, among these St. Denis with his head in his hand, St. Sebastian pierced with arrows, and others. The upper series, on a smaller scale, represents allegorical subjects, some of which are treated in a curiously homely and practical manner, for instance, the figure of Adam holding the apple in his hand with a look as much as to say, "This is what has ruined me;" Eve, in the next compartment, looks somewhat nonchalant, rather a coquette than a penitent. In some of these Biblical scenes the figures are naively dressed in mediaeval garb, but many of them have great beauty and pathos. The under-pieces of the seats, cornices, and sides are decorated with all kinds of drolleries, and not a few coarse subjects, such as a man catching hold of a pig by its tail, faces ludicrously distorted, three heads in one, a dog setting its back at a wild boar, &c. One corner-piece represents the first Abbots of St. Claude building the Abbey, and comical little devils perched on trees pelting them with stones. The whole is a wonderful piece of work, full of originality, strength, and real artistic feeling.

The triptych, imputed to Holbein, may well be his work. The sacristan's little son took me to the upper chapel, where it hangs quite lost upon those below. It is as beautiful as its altarpiece in wood; the three central compartments filled with large figures of the Abbot of St. Claude and his Apostles; below, on a small scale, the Last Supper, and other subjects, treated in a masterly manner. The colours are still bright, though the whole is in a terribly dirty state, and below the central figure is a coronal of the loveliest little cherub heads. Unfortunately, no photograph is to be had of this triptych, and it is hung in a very obscure place. These two works of art, each a gem in its way, are all that remains of the once puissant and magnificent Abbey of St. Claude. Having completed a leisurely inspection, I quietly took a chair behind my companions, for fear of disturbing their devotions. I found, however, that these were over long ago, and that, though in a devout position, they were discussing fashion and gossip as a matter of course! Twice, during my visits to the Cathedral, I had found thirty Dominicans at vespers, and I was informed afterwards that these were poor students who were maintained and prepared for the office of teachers at the expense of a rich young Abbe of St. Claude. It happened that I fell into conversation with this young Abbe in a photographic shop, and found him very agreeable and instructed. It seems a pity he could not find some better means of employing his fortune.

In that same photograph shop were hung photographs of the Pope and Gram-betta, side by side, the shop-keeper acting, I presume, on the principle of one of George Eliot's characters, who had to vote "as a family man." Doubtless, being the father of a family, this stationer felt it expedient to be agreeable to both parties, Clerical and Republican. St. Claude, like the other towns I have passed through in the heart of the Jura, is eminently Republican, and a very intelligent workman told me that Catholic parents were compelled to send their children to the lay Commu-nal Schools, instead of to the Freres Ignorantins, because with the latter they learn nothing. Many of these Freres Ignorantins I saw here, and graceless figures they are. One can but pity them, for as lay instruction is fast superseding clerical, what will soon be their raison d'etre?

There is no Protestant organization at St. Claude, but most likely it will soon come. English Protestants must never forget that money is sorely needed by the struggling Protestant communities in France; and that, without money, schools, hospitals, and churches cannot be built. At present, as I have before mentioned, trade is at a low ebb, but the projected railway connecting St. Claude with Nantua will give new development to its industries, and also throw open a new and beauti-ful pleasure-ground to travellers. My friends entrusted me to the care of an intel-ligent workman in order to see the manufactures of the "articles de St. Claude," viz.: pipes, toys, inlaid work, and carved objects in bone, ivory, &c. We saw small blocks of the so called bois de bruyere, as they come straight from the Pyrenees, which are cut about the length of pipes, and are worked up partly by hand and partly by ma-chinery. Women, girls, and children are largely employed with the turning lathes, and in many other processes; I saw a woman polishing handles of the toys known as cup and ball; also box-wood tops being turned, and rules and measures being made; the thin blades of folding rules are made with marvellous rapidity, as had need to be the case, seeing how low is the price at which these and other goods of this kind are sold by the gross for foreign markets. Having gone through the various workshops of a large manufactory, my companion conducted me to see the handwork done at home. We found a young artist, for so we must call him, at work in a clean little room opening into a garden, and much he told us of interest. He said that he could only earn five francs a day, and this by dint of hard work, carving two dozen pipes a day, at the rate of two and a half francs per dozen. These vine-leaves, flowers, arabesques, and other patterns are done with marvellous swiftness and dexterity, and entirely according to the fancy of the moment, and for his artistic education he had paid high. All the best workmen, he told me, were going to Paris in order to get better pay and shorter hours of labour. Strikes here are out of the question, as there are no Trades' Unions and associations in order to raise the price of labour. Meantime wages decrease, and the cost of living augments. A gloomy picture he drew of trade prospects at St. Claude, that is to say, from the workman's point of view. The arts of turnery, inlaid work, carving in wood and ivory, have long been peculiar to St. Claude, though when first they were introduced is not exactly known. First of all, it was the box-wood of the Jura that these rustic artists put into requisition, then buffalo and stags' horns, lastly, ivory, vegetable ivory, and foreign woods. The part of the box-wood used chiefly is an intermediate part between the root and the stem called la loupe, or racine de bruyere; whilst the red wood used for pipes is the root of a heath common in the Pyrenees, which has the peculiar quality of resisting heat, and is free from odour or taste. So great is the division of labour in the manufacture of the St. Claude wares that it is said there are three thousand different processes in turnery alone! A child's top, even though of the simplest, goes through a great number of stages before being finished for the markets. Chaplets are also manufactured largely, and is the earliest branch of industry, dating from the Middle Ages. Snuffboxes in inlaid wood, ivory, and bone are made in great quantities, also rules and measures, spectacle cases, napkin rings, salad spoons and forks, and other articles of the kind. Four-fifths of the St. Claude wares are exported; an especial kind of pipes being made expressly for the English market. It is stated that, during the general Exhibition at Hyde Park in 1862, many Frenchmen brought home, as English curiosities, the elegantly carved pipes of St. Claude! The United States of America also import great quantities of these pipes. In the last American war, there was hardly a soldier who did not possess a pipe manufactured in the little city in the Jura mountains. There is also another branch of industry more fascinating still, which is peculiar to St. Claude and the neighbouring village of Septmoncel; but, perhaps, I am indiscreet in speaking of it, so dire is the temptation it holds out to the traveller. As you stroll along these quiet streets, your eyes are attracted here and there by open boxes of what appears, at first sight, to be large beads, but which are in reality gems and precious stones; amethysts, emeralds, sapphires, topazes, and diamonds, lie here in dazzling little heaps, and if you are a connoisseur in such matters, and have not spent all your money on the way, you may carry home with you one of the most delightful of all souvenirs to be set at pleasure. Diamond polishing and gem-cutting are largely carried on here, but form, more especially, the industry of Septmoncel, a little village in the mountains, a few miles distant from St. Claude. Several thousand souls depend for daily bread on this delicate occupation, which none know how long has been peculiar to the inhabitants of Septmoncel, and their monopoly is only rivalled by the diamond polishers of Amsterdam. These ateliers are well worth visiting. Besides diamonds and precious stones, rock crystal, and various kinds of imitations, and paste jewellery are here worked up; also jasper, agate, malachite, cornelian, lapis-lazuli, jet, &c. The work is done by the piece, and the whole family of the lapidary is generally employed.

A journey of political propaganda had just been accomplished in these mountain regions, and the well-known writer Jean Mace, accompanied by some leading Republicans, among these Victor Poupin, editor of the useful little series of works called L'Instruction Republicaine and La Bibliotheque Democratique. At St. Claude the occasion was turned into a general fete; the place was decorated with tri-coloured flags, a banquet was held, and the whole proceedings passed off to the satisfaction of all but the cures. In one of the little mountain towns, the cure preached in the pulpit against the sous-prefet and his wife, because, upon one of these occasions, before taking part in the Republican fete, they did not attend mass.

Travelling in the Jura will, doubtless, one day be made easy and pleasant, and, perhaps, become the fashion. As it is, in spite of the glorious weather, no tourist is seen here, and the diligence to Nantua was almost empty. It is a superb drive of five or six hours by the valley of the Bienne and Oyonnaz, a little town which is the seat of an important comb-manufactory. Keeping by the river, here so intensely clear that every pebble may be seen in the water, we gradually quit the severer characteristics of the Jura for its milder and more smiling aspects. Traversing a savage gorge, we soon come to the marble quarries of Chassal and Molinges, also, at the former place, ochre quarries. The red and yellow marbles of the Jura, so richly veined and ornamental, will, doubtless, constitute a great source of wealth in the Department as soon as there are improved means of transport. In that rich marble region, we find only box trees and other dwarf shrubs, with abundance of romantic little cascades, grottoes, rivulets, and mountain springs. All this bit of country, indeed, is most interesting, picturesquely, industrially, and geologically, and on this perfect day, the second of October, every feature is beautified by the weather; large cumuli dropping violet shadows on the hills, deep ravines showing intensest purple, golden mists veiling the verdant valleys. We are soon in a pastoral country, and, as we pass chalets perched on some far off ridge, little girls run down from the mountain sides with letters in their hands, which the conductor drops into his little box attached to the diligence. We are, in fact, the travelling post-office. How laborious the life of the peasant-farmer is here, we may judge from the hard work being done by the women and girls. In some cases, they guide the team whilst the man behind holds the plough, in others they are digging up potatoes, or gathering in their little crop of maize. All the women seem to be out of doors and sunburnt, toil-worn looking creatures they are, though they wear an expression of contentment, or rather res-ignation. The potato crop, on which these rural populations so largely depend for winter food, is fortunately good and abundant, and little else but potato and maize seem to be grown here. The villages we pass through have a dirty and neglected appearance; but beggars are nowhere encountered, and, at the entrance of each, we see the inscription, "Mendicity is forbidden in the Department of the Jura."

CHAPTER XII.
NANTUA AND THE CHURCH OF BRON.

It was evening when we reached the little railway-station of La Cluse, and exquisite indeed was the twilight drive to Nantua. The crimson glories of sunset were still flaming in the west, and reflected in the limpid lake, whilst a silvery crescent moon rose slowly above the dark purple mountains framing in the picture. A delicious scene this, and wonderfully contrasted to the sombre splendour of St. Claude, tenderest allegro after stateliest adagio maestoso, droppings of pearly rain after heavy thunder-claps. Nantua must be seen from above its interesting Romanesque old church to be appreciated. It lies at the end of a mountain gorge, black with pines from summit to base, the transparent fairy-like lake opening beyond, shut in with violet hills.

No less delightful is the walk to La Cluse alongside the lake, an umbrageous avenue, the shadows of which are grateful this hot June-like October day. Through a light screen of foliage you look across the blue waters upon bluer hills, and still bluer sky. Nantua, in spite of its smiling appearance, is inevitably doomed one day to destruction, Straight over against the town impends a huge mass of loosened rock, which, so authorities predict, must sooner or later slide down, crushing any thing with which it comes in contact. People point to the enemy with nonchalance, saying, "Yes, the rock will certainly fall at some time or other, and destroy a great part of the town, but not perhaps in our time." Be this as it may, the gigantic fragment of rock hanging so menacingly over Nantua, is a curious object of contemplation.

I fell into conversation with two nuns belonging to the Order of St. Charles, and I wish I could delineate the hideousness of their costumes, and the unmitigated ugliness of their general appearance. Their dress consisted of a plain black gown with round cape and close fitting hood, on each side of which projected black gauze flaps extended on wires, shading their withered, ill-favoured countenances, and making them look indeed more like female inquisitors, ogres, or Witches of Endor than human beings. I never saw human nature made so uninviting, and I could fancy the terror inspired by these awful figures, with their bat-like flaps, in the tender minds of the little children entrusted to their care. It was edifying to hear these holy women discourse upon the Paris Exhibition, which it is hardly necessary to say the clerical party throughout France was bound to consider a failure. Alike the highest and the lowest, bishop and parish priest, were determined in their own minds that the Exhibition, as a display of rehabilitated France under a Republican Government, should fail altogether, and come to some conspicuously bad end. The very reverse had happened, yet here were two women of age, experience, and some intelligence coolly talking of this terrible failure of the Exhibition, financially and otherwise, the bad effect upon trade generally, and so forth.

I take the railway from Bourg to La Cluse, a mile from the town, and a marvellous piece of railway engineering is this short journey, veritable Alpine ascent in a railway-carriage, scaling perpendicular mountain sides by means of the steam-engine! The train curls round the mountain as the Jura roads are made to do, high above an awful gorge, in the midst of which runs the River Ain, emerald-green irradiated by diamond-like flashes of cascade and torrent. When we have accomplished this aerial bit of travel--it is very like being up in a balloon--we suddenly lose alike mountain, river, and ravine, all the world of enchantment in which I had been living for weeks past, to find ourselves in the region of prose and common-place! In other words, we were in the wide, highly cultivated plain of La Bresse. At Bourg-en-Bresse I halted, as everyone else must do, in order to see its famous Church of Brou. The Church was built in consequence of a vow made by Margaret of Burgundy, that if her husband, Philibert the Second, Duke of Savoy, was healed from injuries received in the hunt, she would erect a church and found a monastery of the Order of St. Benoit. The Duke recovered, but his wife died before accomplishing her work, which was, however, carried out by her daughter-in-law, Margaret of Austria, wife of Philibert le Beau. She summoned for this purpose all the best artists of the time to Bourg, and the church begun in 1506 was finished in 1532, under the direction of Loys von Berghem.

This spirited and imperious Margaret of Austria, known as Margot la Flamande, played an important part in history, as readers of Michelet's eloquent seventh volume know. She adored her second husband, the handsome Philibert, and owed all her life a grudge against France, on account of having been, as a child, promised in marriage to Charles VIII., and afterwards supplanted for political reasons by the no less imperious Anne of Brittany. Aunt and first instructress of Charles V., King of Spain and Emperor of Germany, she is regarded by Michelet as the founder of the House of Austria, and one of the chief agents in humiliating France by means of the Treaty of Cambrai. Margaret of Austria, Anne of Brittany, Louise of Savoy, mother of Francis I., writes the historian, "cousant, filant, lisant, ces trois fatales Parques ont tissu les maux de l'Europe" (sewing, spinning, reading, these three fatal Parcae were the misfortune of Europe), and the student of French history will follow the career of all three with interest after the clue here given them. Margaret, bitter, vindictive, and designing, seems to have had one poetic thread in her life only, namely, her passion for her husband, whose beauty lives in marble before us.

The Church of Brou--magnificent case for these gems of monumental art--cost seven millions of francs, and the combined labours of the best living architects and artists of the time, may be considered as the last efflorescence of Gothic architecture, for the spirit of the Renaissance was already making itself felt. It is less, however, the church, in spite of its rich exterior and elegant proportions, that travellers will come to see than the exquisite mausoleum of the choir, each deserving a chapter to itself. You quit the quiet old-fashioned town of Bourg, and after a walk of twenty minutes, come suddenly on the church, standing in the suburb, or as it seems, indeed, in the open country. A sacristan is at hand to unlock the door of the choir, but it is best to give him his fee in advance, and tell him to return in an hour; generally speaking, other strangers are coming and going, in which case such a precaution is not necessary, but it is impossible to enjoy this artistic treat with a guide hovering about you, doling out pieces of stale information, and impatiently awaiting to be paid. The choir is screened off from the nave by a rich, although somewhat heavy rood-loft, and great is the contrast between the two portions of the church; in the first, all is subdued, quiet in tone, and refreshing; in the last, the eye is troubled by too much light, there is no stained glass to soften down the brilliant sunshine of this fine October day, and, although the architectural proportions of the entire building are graceful and on a vast scale, the beholder is much less delighted than he ought to be on this account. In fact the effect is dazzling; but how different are our sensations when once on the other side of the richly sculptured rood-loft! Here the impression is one of peerless beauty, without a shadow of disillusion or the slightest drawback to aesthetic enjoyment, except one, and that very trifling. These three mausoleums are so well defended against possible iconoclasts that the thick, closely set iron bars almost prevent us from seeing the lower part of the three tombs, and, in two cases, these are as interesting as any. Surely in the present day such measures are unnecessary! It may be mentioned that the church and tombs narrowly escaped destruction during the great Revolution, and the world is indebted for their safety to the public spirit of one of the civil authorities, who filled the interior with hay, securely fastened the doors, and put outside the conspicuous inscription: Propriete Nationale. But for these prompt measures, the beautiful and unique treasures contained in the Church of Brou would, without doubt, have shared the fate of so many others during that awful epoch.

The three tombs are those of Philibert le Beau, Duke of Savoy, of Margaret, Duchess of Burgundy, his mother, and of Margaret of Austria, his wife. They are chiselled in Carrara marble, and are the combined work of Michel Colomb, Jean Perreal, called Jean de Paris, and Conrad Meyt.[4] The central tomb is that of Philibert, who, like his wife, is represented twice, the upper figure that of the Duke when alive, the lower delineating death. This monument is perhaps the most splendid of all, although there are especial beauties to be found in the other two, and each is deserving of long and careful study.

Above, therefore, we have the Prince in all the glory of life and pomp of state; below, in the cold bareness and nakedness of death, a contrast highly artistic and touching at the same time. The iron rails already alluded to only hide the lower division of the tomb, so that we see the upper part in all its splendour. The Prince, wearing his ducal cap and dress, reposes on a couch, the cushion supporting his head being covered with delicate sculptures, his feet resting on a lion recumbent, his hands clasped, his face slightly turned towards Margaret of Austria, his wife. On each side, little lovely naked boys, geniuses, loves, cherubs--call them what we will--support his helmet and gloves, and charming statuettes after the same dainty pattern stand at each corner of the sarcophagus supporting his shield and various

---

4 Consult on this subject "Monographie de l'Eglise de Brou," par MM. Didron et Dupasquier.

pieces of armour. Underneath, on a slab of black marble, lies the figure of the dead Prince, the finely modelled limbs only partially draped, the long hair curling round the bare shoulder, the beautiful face turned, as in the first instance, towards the image of his wife--pose, expression, design, all combining to make up an exquisite whole. This second figure is a master-piece, and no less masterly are the Sibyls and other figures which surround it, each statuette deserving the most careful study, each, in fact, a little gem. The frame-work of this noble monument is of rich Gothic design, too elaborate, perhaps, to please the fastidious critic, but deliciously imaginative, and finished as far as artistic finish can go. To the right of the Prince is the tomb of Marguerite of Burgundy, his mother, a hardly less sumptuous piece of work than the first, and superbly framed in by Gothic decorative sculptures, statuettes, arabesques, flowers, and heraldic designs. The little mourning figures or pleureuses, each in its graceful niche, are wonderfully beautiful, and for the most part veiled, whilst the artist's fancy has been allowed to run riot in the ornamentation surrounding them. The Princess wears her long ducal mantle and crown, and at her feet reposes a superb greyhound. The third tomb, that of Marguerite of Austria, the wife of Philibert, is in some respects the richest of the three, being almost bewildering in elaborateness of detail and abundance of ornament. It is divided into two compartments; in the upper, we have the living figure of a beautiful woman in the flower of life, richly dressed; in the lower, we have the same after death, the long hair rippling in curls to her waist, the slender feet showing from under the drapery, the expression that of majestic calm and solemnity. We have here the simplicity and nakedness of death in close proximity with the gorgeousness and magnificence of art--art under one of its most sumptuous aspects, art in its fullest and most poetic moods. All thoughtful observers must come to the conclusion that lovely and artistic as is the frame-work of this last figure, each tiniest detail being a marvel both of design and execution, it is, perhaps, not quite in harmony with the rest. It is, indeed, somewhat overcharged with ornament. Be this as it may, the mausoleums in the Church of Brou will ever remain in the memory as one of those exquisite and unique art experiences that form an epoch in our inner history. For what, indeed, avails art at all, if it is a thing of minor importance in life, a half joy, a half consolation, a second or inferior impression to be effaced by anything new that comes in our way? It was pitiable to see parties of two or three French tourists rush into the choir with the sacristan, spend five minutes in glancing at the treasures before them, then hurry away, not dreaming of what they have failed to see, only dimly conscious of having seen something. It is curious that in 1856 the lead coffins containing the remains of Philibert and the two Duchesses were discovered in a crypt under that part of the choir where the mausoleums stand. The inscriptions on all three were perfectly legible, and left no doubt as to identity; the skeletons were placed in new coffins, and re-interred with religious ceremony. Other crypts were discovered, but these had evidently been spoliated.

Before quitting these mausoleums and their exquisite possessions of pleureuses, geniuses, Sibyls, and the rest, it may be worth while to remind the reader that, according to the most learned of the Romans, there were ten Sibyls, viz.:--1. Persica, 2. Libyssa, 3. Delphica, 4. Cumaea, 5. Erythraea, 6. Samia, 7. Cumana, who brought the book to Tarquin, 8. Hellespontica, 9. Phrygia, 10. Tiburs, by name Albunea, worshipped at Tiber as a goddess. Thus Varro categorizes the Sibyls, and besides these we hear of a Hebrew, a Chaldaean, a Babylonian, an Egyptian, a Sardian Sibyl, and some others. Other writers considerably reduce this number, three being that most usually accepted, and Salmasius, the most learned man that ever lived, summed up the various theories concerning these mysterious beings with the words: "There is nothing on which ancient writers more widely differ than as to the age, number, and country of the Sibyls."

There is little to see in the Church of Brou besides these mausoleums, and nothing in Bourg itself, except the fine bronze statue to Bichat, by David d'Angers. The great anatomist is represented in the act of oscultation, the patient being a child, standing between his knees. It is a monument alike worthy of the artist and his subject, another instance of that dignified realism for which David d'Angers was so remarkable. There is, however, some doubt as to Bichat's birth-place; Lons-le-Saunier, as I have before mentioned, contesting the honour with Bourg. On the principle that two monuments to a great man are better than none at all, each place claims the honour.

The night mail-express from Geneva whirled me in about ten hours to Paris, and the next morning I found myself in what, after the matchless atmosphere of the Jura, seemed murkiness, although the day was fine and the sky cloudless. I had thus, with hardly an important deviation from the plan originally laid down, accomplished my journey in Eastern France, but with a success, in one respect, impossible to anticipate. Accustomed as I am to French amiability and hospitality, I was yet unprepared for such a reception as that accorded to me throughout every stage of my travels. All hearts were open to me; everyone wanted to do the honours of his beloved "patrie"--using the word in its local rather than national sense--to be serviceable, kind, accommodating. Thus it happened that my holiday rambles in Franche-Comté were so far novel, that they may be said to have been accomplished without hotels or guidebooks; for the most part, my time being spent in friends' houses, and my itineraries being the best possible, namely, the oral information of interested natives of every place I passed through. This is, indeed, the way in which all countries, and especially France, should be seen, for, without a sympathetic knowledge of her people and their ways of life, we lose the most interesting feature in French travel. Travellers who only see the outside of things in foreign countries, indeed, may be compared to those who gaze upon a skeleton, instead of the living form, warm with life, sympathy, and beauty. Old France, as studied in her glorious monuments, whether Gallic, Merovingian, Mediaeval, or Renaissance, pales in interest before the New, that France which alone has taught the world the lesson of Equality, and is teaching us every day what misfortunes may be overcome by a noble people, inspired with true patriotism, allied to democratic feeling. In Republican France, now, who can doubt? and I am all the more thankful here to be able to bear witness to the unanimity, prosperity, and marvellous development found in the different strata of French social life. There are, without doubt, blots on this bright picture; but none can deny that the more we learn to know France the more we admire and love her, and that, if the richest and most beautiful country in the world, it is also the one in which happiness and well-being are most generally diffused. We are accustomed to regard France in the light of a parable to other nations, but, if her sorrows and retributions have taught them much, at least her successes and triumphs have taught them more. She has lately shown herself greater even in the hour of her prosperity than in that of evil fortune, the highest praise to be accorded alike to nations as to individuals. Honour then to all who have helped in bringing about these great results, whether in the humblest or loftiest walks of life, and may I be the means of inducing scores of travellers to follow in my footsteps, and judge for themselves whether I have drawn too glowing a picture! Of one thing they may be certain--namely, that they will be welcomed wherever they go, if led thither in a sympathetic spirit, although, perhaps, not many may have the like good fortune with myself, each stage of my journey being marked by delightful acquaintances and friendships, binding me still closer to La Belle France and her glorious Republic!

APPENDIX.

ITINERARIES.--OUTLINES OF FRANC-COMTOIS HISTORY. NOTES ON THE GEOLOGY OF THE JURA.

For the benefit of pedestrians, and these will most enjoy the country I have described, I adjoin some itineraries, more detailed than I was enabled to make my own. Hardy travellers will be well satisfied, in most instances, with the wayside inns they will find, and one advantage of travelling in Franche-Comte--at least, up to the present time--is its inexpensiveness. The chief outlay is in carriage hire, and those who can endure the diligence, or, better still, can accomplish most of their journeys on foot, where the railway is not available, will not only see the country to the best advantage, but at a very trifling cost. The excursions, or rather group of excursions, here mentioned, are such as may be accomplished in a few days from the town given as a starting point.

I. Besancon to Alaise and the valley of Nans. Departure by way of the route de Beure. The river Loue is crossed at Cleron. From Amancey ascend the plateau above Coulans, where a view is obtained of the oppidum of Alaise (supposed by some authorities to be the Alesia of Julius Caesar). Descend to the mill of Chiprey, follow the right bank of the Lison to Nans. At Nans, visit the Grotte Sarrazine, the source of the Lison, and the Pont du Diable. Ascend the fortress of St. Agne for the sake of the panorama; ancient dwellings of the Gauls to be seen at Chatillon, also tombs at Foure, see also the Cascade of the Gour de Couche, the Col de la Langutine, descend by way of the Taudeur to the plain of Myon, bounding the western side of the Alesia, i.e., the Alesia of some authorities.

II. Luxeuil (Luxovium) in Haute Saone. Celebrated from the ancient times for its ferruginous springs. Here visit the Roman remains, mediaeval houses, the town for the sake of the view. Make excursions into the valleys of the Vosges.

III. Vesoul and Gray, departure from Besancon by way of the charming valley of Ognon. See the Chateau de la Roche, turned into a school of agriculture, the sculptures in Vesoul church, its old streets, and pretty gardens. Visit the Port sur Saone (Portus Abucinus). At Gray visit the Hotel de Ville, the house of Simon d'Ancier, maitre-d'hotel of the Connetable de Bourbon. Visit the Abbey of Pesmes which contains some fine Renaissance work, the ancient Abbey of Acey, the Chateau de Balancon, Marnay, ancient domain of the Joinvilles, Ruffey--Roman city destroyed by the Vandals.

IV. From Besancon to Pontanier (Abiolica)--a beautiful bit of railway. The Doubs is crossed twice, when views are obtained of Arguel and Montferrand, and the modern chateaux of Torpes and Thoraise. The Loue is crossed at Mouchard; fine view of the ruins of Vaugrenant. After leaving Mouchard, the traveller enjoys a succession of vast prospects of the vineyard region of the Jura--Aiglepierre, Marnoz, Arbois, &c. After the vines, come the pinewoods and the splendid forest of Joux. After the pinewoods generally come the peat-fields, or tourbieres, of Chaux d'Arlier, traversed by two rivers which here meet, the Doubs and the Drugeon. Lastly, Pontarlier is reached, eight hundred and seventy yards above the level of the sea, anciently a confederation of nineteen villages, called la baroichage.

V. From Besancon to Dole. Four routes are here open to the traveller; 1st. The Roman road leading formerly from Vesontio to Cabillorum; 2nd. the route de Paris; 3rd. the railway--Dijon line; 4th. the canal, from the Rhone to the Rhine. All these ways of communication follow the valley of the Doubs. The great forges of Fraisans, and the Roman station of Crusinia, are to be seen on the way. To the right of this is a huge mass of granite in the midst of the Jurassic formation. Dole is the second city in Franche-Comte, and houses are to be seen there. The public library is also worth a visit.

VI. The fortress of Joux and the Swiss routes. Two fortresses protect the Swiss frontiers, Joux and Larmont. The former merits a visit. The cells are seen in which Toussaint l'Ouverture, Mirabeau, the poet Kleist, and other illustrious prisoners were confined. In the neighbourhood of Joux are high mountain peaks from which magnificent views are to be had. Many interesting excursions to be made in this neighbourhood.

VII. The Falls of the Doubs, Morteau, and Montbenoit. Start from Morteau, visit the Falls and Lakes, also the Cols de Roches. Proceed to Montbenoit by the river Doubs. See the splendid rock at Entreroches. The church of Montbenoit is one of the historic monuments of France; here are to be seen statuettes and sculptures in wood, the work of Florentine artists in the sixteenth century, employed by the Abbe Carondelet, friend of Raphael and Erasmus.

VIII. Baume-les-Dames. By rail and road from Besancon or Montbeliard, passing the picturesque valley of the Doubs, rich in charming landscape and historic associations. Ruins of the Chateaux of Montfaucon and Vaite, to be seen on the way. At Baume-les-Daines, visit the ancient Abbey Church, now turned into a public granary, also the valley of the Cuisancin, last, the Glaciere de la Grace-Dieu, a natural phenomenon of great beauty and interest.

IX. From Andelot to Orgelet. The railway takes you to Champagnole. From thence take a carriage to the Source of the Ain, and Les Planches, visiting by the way the church of Sirod. Drive also to Nozeroy and the valley of Miege, and visit the parish church, which is full of statuettes. Thence proceed to St. Laurent by way of the fall of the Lemme, the Lake of Bonlieu, and the ruins of the Chartreuse. From Morez ascend the fortress of the Rousses, and follow the road to Dole, by the valley des Dappes; splendid views of Switzerland. From St. Claude is a public conveyance to Orgelet, Roman ruins (ville d'Antres) to be seen on the way, also the Chartreuse of Vaucleuse, and the Chateau of the Tour-de-Meix. Railway at Orgelet.

*   *   *   *   *

These Itineraries can be varied almost ad infinitum, and we only give an indication of the variety of walks and drives to be found in this most "spazierlich" country. The knapsack tourists, of course, have always the advantage in every way.

As a rule, no one ever reads anything when travelling, but, for the benefit of those conscientious travellers who like to do things systematically, I will mention one or two books that may usefully supplement Murray or Joanne. Two of these, to be picked up on the way, are really school-books, but are so crammed full of information, and so entertaining, that no tourist in Franche-Comte can afford to pass them by. The first, "La Franche-Comte et le pays de Montbeliard," is a succinct and admirably digested little history of the country. Its author, M. Castan, the learned librarian of Besancon, gives, in a small compass, what is not easy to get at elsewhere, enough, indeed, of history for all ordinary purposes. A second and no less admirable compendium of information for travellers in the Jura, is the, so-called, "Lectures Jurassiennes," a little work compiled for elementary schools, but in reality "Half-hours with the best Franc-Comtois authors," who treat of the general features, products, climate, &c., of the Jura, as well as of the people; their legendary lore, habits of life, and general characteristics. A delightful little volume this, giving passages from Lamartine, who just missed being a native of the Jura himself, from Xavier Marinier, author of "Souvenirs of Franche-Comte," and from Charles Nodier, that gifted and charming writer, to whom the very name of his native province was a magic spell, awakening all kinds of joyous and glowing recollections. Those who find amusement in a popular historical novel may consult "Le Medecin des Pauvres," in which they will find delineations of the most romantic scenery of the Jura, interspersed with thrilling incidents. For botanists, there is an admirable Handbook, in two volumes, "La Flore Jurassienne," to be found in every town by the way; lastly, for special information, "Roussel's Dictionnaire Geographique, Historique, et Statistique;" these two last may be consulted in any local library by the way. Students of geology will find useful information in Joanne's little "Geographies Departementales." Excellent maps are to be had everywhere. Real lovers of literature, however, will content themselves with the delightful writings of Charles Nodier, and to this fascinating story-teller I am indebted, not only for many delightful hours in my study, but for the pleasure of travelling in Franche-Comte myself, and afterwards introducing it to my country-people. Of him, poet, novelist, as of a critic, naturalist, philologist, essayist, still more illustrious writer of our own, it might be said, "Nihil tetigit quod non ornavit."

The history of Franche-Comte, which M. Castan gives in a nutshell, may be greatly simplified by following his division into periods. Beginning therefore from the earliest period down to the present time. The following are the principal facts, simplified by this historic arrangement.

1st Period. Sequanian. 115-147 B.C.--The province successively called Sequania, Haute Bourgogne, Comte de Bourgogne and Franche-Comte--of which the larger portion actually forms the three Departments of the Jura, Haute Saone, and the Doubs--was early recognized as one of the most important strategical and natural divisions of ancient Gaul. The Sequani, by way of rewarding them for their aid against the Cimbri and Teutons, were received as friends and allies of the Roman people. When Caesar entered upon his conquests, he found two rival parties in Gaul, the Aedui and the Sequani, the latter, being oppressed by Ariovistus, besought his aid. Caesar vanquished Ariovistus, and took up his winter-quarters in the Sequanian territory, 56 B.C. The general rising of Gaul was quelled after seven years' struggle, and the surrender of the heroic Auvergnat chief, Vercingetorix, at Alesia--according to some authorities, Alaise in Franche-Comte, to others, Alise la Reine, in Auvergne. This happened in 47 B.C. (see Julius Caesar's "Gallic War.")

II. Roman Period, 47 B.C. 407 A.D. The Roman Emperors now attempted, in so far as possible, to denationalize the ancient kingdom of the Gauls, transforming not only laws and language, but manners and customs. Roman gods took the place of so-called Druidic rites. Roman roads spread like a net-work throughout the country, sumptuous edifices were erected at Vesontio (Besancon), and Epomanduodarum (Maudeure, Doubs). The thermal and ferruginous springs of Luxovium (Luxueil), and Salinae (Salins), attracted the Roman world of fashion. Wines of the Jura found their way to luxurious tables of Rome and Athens. The brave Sabinus made an attempt to shake off the Roman yoke, and his virtuous and heroic wife, by her devotion, shines among the heroines of her country. (See Thierry's "Histoire des Gaulois.") Besancon was made capital of Sequania, and embellished, under the reign of Marcus Aurelius with amphitheatre, forum, triumphal arch, theatre, &c. Christianity made its first appearance in the country. Two emissaries of Irenaeus, Bishop of Lyons, suffered martyrdom in the Theatre of Besancon, 212 A.D. Sequania, including the present Franche-Comte, was created a military province, under the title of Provincia Maxima Sequanorum. Under Constantine, Christian churches were built in many places, and the Basilica, now the Cathedral of Besancon, begun.

III. Burgundian Period, 407-534. The Burgundians, having aided the Romans to free the Sequanian territory from the Huns under Attila, settled there, 435-471; the land being divided among them and its former owners. Monasteries were first founded about this time, notably the Abbey of Condat, now St. Claude. Gondioc, King of the Burgundians, owned the actual countries now included in Franche-

Comte; besides Burgundy, La Bresse, Savoy, Dauphine, and Provence. The Franks seized the kingdom from the descendants of Gondioc after a Burgundian occupation of two hundred years.

IV. Frankish Period, 534-711. The ancient territory of Gondioc was now divided among the descendants of Clovis, who built many monasteries and abbeys, among these Baume-les-Dames, and that of Luxueil, Haute Saone. On the death of Charles Martel, a new division took place, and Burgundy, including Franche-Comte, fell to the lot of Pepin le Bref.

V. Carlovingian Period, 741-879. Under Charlemagne, the clergy rose to pre-eminent importance, and great privileges were accorded to religious foundations, &c.

VI. Feudal Period, 879-1038. Three hosts of invaders ravaged the country, the Normans, the Germans, and the Huns. The kingdom of Burgundy, including Franche-Comte, was incorporated with the German Empire in the early part of the eleventh century.

VII. Sacerdotal Period, 1038-1148. A darker and more troublous time hardly appears in French history. The petty sovereigns of the different principalities into which Franche-Comte had been divided were engaged in perpetual struggles with their spiritual chiefs. Hugh, Archbishop of Besancon, ruled with kingly authority. Ten Cistercian Abbeys were founded. Land was cleared in the most solitary places for the purpose of building monasteries, notably at Morteau and Mouthe. Beatrix, heiress of Count Raimond III, was shut up in a tower by her uncle, and liberated by Frederic Barbarossa.

VIII. German Period, 1148-1248. Frederic Barbarossa having married Beatrix, Franche-Comte became an appanage of the German Empire. The Chateau of Dole was made the imperial residence and the seat of Government. On the death of the Emperor and Beatrix, the heritage of Franche-Comte was contested by Count Otho I. and Etienne d'Auxonne. Successive wars between the rival families ravaged the country for many years.

IX. Communal Period, 1248-1330. Jean de Chalons, to whom the heritage had accrued, granted charters of disenfranchisement to many towns, Salins, Ornans, and others. The Commune of Besancon was definitely founded, and it became an independent city, under the protectorate of the German Empire. Otho IV., Emperor of Germany, made over the country to Philippe le Bel, King of France, who, after five years, subdued the refractory Franc-Comtois, and greatly benefited the country by the introduction of French customs and forms of legislation. Jeanne, daughter of Philippe le Bel, peacefully governed the province for five years, and introduced the manufacture of cloth at Gray. In 1330, Franche-Comte fell to the share of the eldest daughter of Jeanne, married to the Duke of Burgundy.

X. Anglo-French Period, 1330-1384. After the treaty of Bretigny, the Grandes Compagniez ravaged Franche-Comte, but were driven back. The nobility entered into an alliance with England, the English King wishing to marry one of his sons with the heiress presumptive of Franche-Comte, great-grand-daughter of the Countess Jeanne. On the negotiations being broken off, the Comtois nobility waged war with England on the side of the French King. It was at this time that the title of Franche-Comte came into use, in order to distinguish the province from that of Burgundy.

XI. Ducal Period, 1381-1477. The Count-Dukes, being engaged in conflict with the clergy and rival nobility, sought the favour of the bourgeoisie by according privileges and titles of nobility. The Comte de Montbeliard passed as a dowry to the house of Wuertemberg in 1397, and remained an appanage of that kingdom till the French Revolution. The power of the aristocracy was considerably diminished at this time, and feudalism broken down by the establishment of the Roman law.

XII. Austrian period, 1477-1556. On the death of Charles le Temeraire, Louis XI. occupied Franche-Comte with a military force, also Burgundy, under the pretext of defending the rights of Marie of Burgundy, daughter of Charles. On the marriage of this princess with Maximilian of Austria, the French were expelled from Franche-Comte. Louis XI., however, re-occupied it; Vesoul, Gray, and Dole were pillaged and burnt. On the death of that King, his successor, Charles VIII., was recognised as sovereign of Franche-Comte by virtue of his proposed marriage with Marguerite, daughter of Marie of Burgundy, wife of Maximilian. He married, however, Anne of Brittany, instead, and the Franc-Comtois thus considered themselves freed from their allegiance to the French crown. Besancon opened its gates to Maximilian, and, in a treaty concluded between the French King and the Emperor, Burgundy reverted to the former, whilst Franche-Comte remained in the hands of the latter. The territorial dowry of Marguerite passed to her brother Philip, afterwards King of

Spain (and father to the celebrated Charles the Fifth), who died, aged twenty-eight. Marguerite then became Regent of Franche-Comte. Under her rule, Protestantism made its first appearance in the provinces. The peasants of Montbeliard, joining the German bands, made raids upon religious houses. Charles the Fifth, on assuming the reins of Government after his aunt Marguerite, continued her policy, and his Keeper of the Seals, the princely Perronet de Granvelle, inaugurated at Besancon, by his splendid patronage of arts and letters, what has justly been called the "Golden Age of Franche-Comte."

XIII. Spanish Period, 1556-1674. Philip II., son of Charles the Fifth, established the Inquisition in Franche-Comte. His reign was a long series of calamities. Henry IV., King of France, marched a large army into the country, but after levying contributions on Besancon, and the smaller towns of the Jura, he signed a treaty, according neutrality to the provinces, and retired (1595). Later, Richelieu sent three armies respectively, into the Saone, the Doubs, and the Jura. St. Claude and Pontarlier were burnt, and the inhabitants destroyed by fire and sword. A great emigration took place, no less than twelve thousand families fleeing to Rome alone. Excepting the four principal towns, Besancon, Salins, Dole, and Gray, the country was almost depopulated. Orders were given to mow down the unripe harvests, in order to subdue the people by famine. At Richelieu's death, neutrality was again accorded to the province, on condition of forty thousand crowns being paid yearly to the crown of France, and French garrisons being maintained at Joux and other places. In the words of a French writer of the period, "The country, at this time, resembled a desert." On the peace of Westphalia, Besancon lost its autonomy, being again placed under the dominion of Spain. Louis XIV. however, having married the daughter of Philip IV. of Spain, claimed Franche-Comte as the dowry of his wife. The great Conde was dispatched on a mission of conquest, the King, in person, headed a besieging army at Gray, and in fifteen days the entire province submitted. By the treaty of Aix-la-Chapelle, Franche-Comte again reverted to Spain, and again had to be conquered. On the declaration of war against France by Spain, the German Empire, Holland, and Lorraine, it put itself on the defensive. The armies of Louis XIV. overran the country. Besancon capitulated, and the King celebrated a Te Deum of victory in the Cathedral of that town in 1674.

It may not be generally known that the Porte St. Martin, in Paris, was erected as a triumphal arch to commemorate this victory. On its principal facade are the words: Ludovico Magno. Vesontione Sequanisque bis capti.

Here the history of Franche-Comte may be said to end, henceforth being merged in that of France. Brief as are these outlines, they will give the reader some idea of the vicissitudes this province has undergone from the earliest times until now; and further details can easily be found elsewhere. From whichever point we may regard it, historically, geographically, or artistically, Franche-Comte must be set down as one of the most interesting portions of France, and none should undertake to visit it without some preconceived notion of what they are going to see.

The Jura is interesting geologically, its series of rocks, of the same age and general lithological structure as the oolitic formations of England, being known as the Jurassic formation. The Jura range is composed of a peculiar kind of limestone abounding in caves, containing stalactital formations and the remains of extinct animals. The highest peak of the Jura rises to 8000 feet. Naturally it is divided into three regions, the plain, the mountain, and the vineyard. The climate, as in most mountainous countries, is rude, winter lasting eight months, on an average with enormous quantities of snow. More than a fourth of the territory is covered with forests, that of La Chaux being one of the finest in France. In the winter the wolves are driven by hunger to the very doors of the villages. The flora of the Jura possesses some singularities, and is especially rich in many districts.

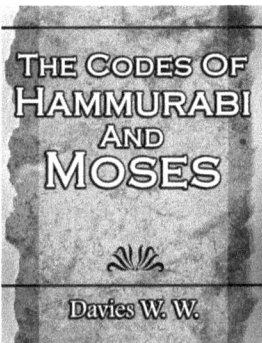

The Codes Of Hammurabi And Moses
W. W. Davies

QTY

The discovery of the Hammurabi Code is one of the greatest achievements of archaeology, and is of paramount interest, not only to the student of the Bible, but also to all those interested in ancient history...

Religion   **ISBN:** *1-59462-338-4*   **Pages:132**

MSRP $12.95

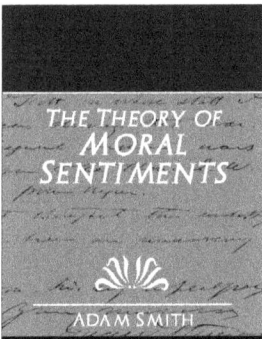

The Theory of Moral Sentiments
Adam Smith

QTY

This work from 1749. contains original theories of conscience amd moral judgment and it is the foundation for systemof morals.

Philosophy   **ISBN:** *1-59462-777-0*   **Pages:536**

MSRP $19.95

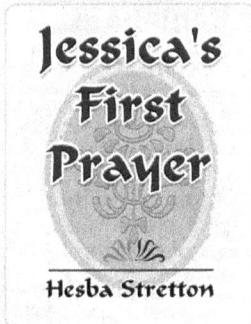

Jessica's First Prayer
Hesba Stretton

QTY

In a screened and secluded corner of one of the many railway-bridges which span the streets of London there could be seen a few years ago, from five o'clock every morning until half past eight, a tidily set-out coffee-stall, consisting of a trestle and board, upon which stood two large tin cans, with a small fire of charcoal burning under each so as to keep the coffee boiling during the early hours of the morning when the work-people were thronging into the city on their way to their daily toil...

Pages:84

Childrens   **ISBN:** *1-59462-373-2*   *MSRP $9.95*

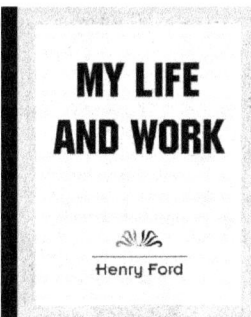

My Life and Work
Henry Ford

QTY

Henry Ford revolutionized the world with his implementation of mass production for the Model T automobile. Gain valuable business insight into his life and work with his own auto-biography... "We have only started on our development of our country we have not as yet, with all our talk of wonderful progress, done more than scratch the surface. The progress has been wonderful enough but..."

Pages:300

Biographies/   **ISBN:** *1-59462-198-5*   *MSRP $21.95*

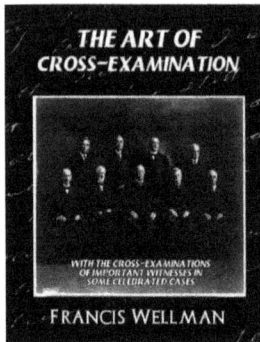

The Art of Cross-Examination
Francis Wellman

QTY

I presume it is the experience of every author, after his first book is published upon an important subject, to be almost overwhelmed with a wealth of ideas and illustrations which could readily have been included in his book, and which to his own mind, at least, seem to make a second edition inevitable. Such certainly was the case with me; and when the first edition had reached its sixth impression in five months, I rejoiced to learn that it seemed to my publishers that the book had met with a sufficiently favorable reception to justify a second and considerably enlarged edition. ..

Reference   ISBN: *1-59462-647-2*

Pages:412

MSRP *$19.95*

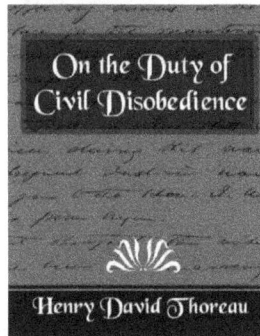

On the Duty of Civil Disobedience
Henry David Thoreau

QTY

Thoreau wrote his famous essay, On the Duty of Civil Disobedience, as a protest against an unjust but popular war and the immoral but popular institution of slave-owning. He did more than write—he declined to pay his taxes, and was hauled off to gaol in consequence. Who can say how much this refusal of his hastened the end of the war and of slavery ?

Law   ISBN: *1-59462-747-9*

Pages:48

MSRP *$7.45*

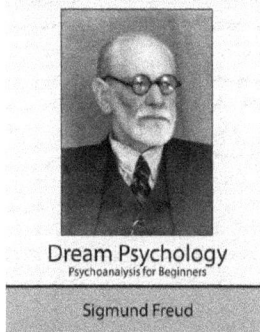

Dream Psychology Psychoanalysis for Beginners
Sigmund Freud

QTY

Sigmund Freud, born Sigismund Schlomo Freud (May 6, 1856 - September 23, 1939), was a Jewish-Austrian neurologist and psychiatrist who co-founded the psychoanalytic school of psychology. Freud is best known for his theories of the unconscious mind, especially involving the mechanism of repression; his redefinition of sexual desire as mobile and directed towards a wide variety of objects; and his therapeutic techniques, especially his understanding of transference in the therapeutic relationship and the presumed value of dreams as sources of insight into unconscious desires.

Psychology   ISBN: *1-59462-905-6*

Pages:196

MSRP *$15.45*

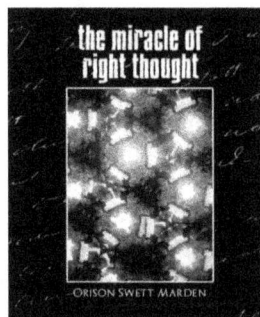

The Miracle of Right Thought
Orison Swett Marden

QTY

Believe with all of your heart that you will do what you were made to do. When the mind has once formed the habit of holding cheerful, happy, prosperous pictures, it will not be easy to form the opposite habit. It does not matter how improbable or how far away this realization may see, or how dark the prospects may be, if we visualize them as best we can, as vividly as possible, hold tenaciously to them and vigorously struggle to attain them, they will gradually become actualized, realized in the life. But a desire, a longing without endeavor, a yearning abandoned or held indifferently will vanish without realization.

Self Help   ISBN: *1-59462-644-8*

Pages:360

MSRP *$25.45*

The Rosicrucian Cosmo-Conception Mystic Christianity by *Max Heindel*　　ISBN: *1-59462-188-8*　**$38.95**
The Rosicrucian Cosmo-conception is not dogmatic, neither does it appeal to any other authority than the reason of the student. It is; not controversial, but is: sent forth in the, hope that it may help to clear...　　New Age/Religion Pages 646

Abandonment To Divine Providence by *Jean-Pierre de Caussade*　　ISBN: *1-59462-228-0*　**$25.95**
"The Rev. Jean Pierre de Caussade was one of the most remarkable spiritual writers of the Society of Jesus in France in the 18th Century. His death took place at Toulouse in 1751. His works have gone through many editions and have been republished...　　Inspirational Religion Pages 400

Mental Chemistry by *Charles Haanel*　　ISBN: *1-59462-192-6*　**$23.95**
Mental Chemistry allows the change of material conditions by combining and appropriately utilizing the power of the mind. Much like applied chemistry creates something new and unique out of careful combinations of chemicals the mastery of mental chemistry...　　New Age Pages 354

The Letters of Robert Browning and Elizabeth Barret Barrett 1845-1846 vol II　　ISBN: *1-59462-193-4*　**$35.95**
by *Robert Browning* and *Elizabeth Barrett*　　Biographies Pages 596

Gleanings In Genesis (volume I) by *Arthur W. Pink*　　ISBN: *1-59462-130-6*　**$27.45**
Appropriately has Genesis been termed "the seed plot of the Bible" for in it we have, in germ form, almost all of the great doctrines which are afterwards fully developed in the books of Scripture which follow...　　Religion/Inspirational Pages 420

The Master Key by *L. W. de Laurence*　　ISBN: *1-59462-001-6*　**$30.95**
In no branch of human knowledge has there been a more lively increase of the spirit of research during the past few years than in the study of Psychology, Concentration and Mental Discipline. The requests for authentic lessons in Thought Control, Mental Discipline and...　　New Age/Business Pages 422

The Lesser Key Of Solomon Goetia by *L. W. de Laurence*　　ISBN: *1-59462-092-X*　**$9.95**
This translation of the first book of the "Lernegton" which is now for the first time made accessible to students of Talismanic Magic was done, after careful collation and edition, from numerous Ancient Manuscripts in Hebrew, Latin, and French...　　New Age/Occult Pages 92

Rubaiyat Of Omar Khayyam by *Edward Fitzgerald*　　ISBN:*1-59462-332-5*　**$13.95**
Edward Fitzgerald, whom the world has already learned, in spite of his own efforts to remain within the shadow of anonymity, to look upon as one of the rarest poets of the century, was born at Bredfield, in Suffolk, on the 31st of March, 1809. He was the third son of John Purcell...　　Music Pages 172

Ancient Law by *Henry Maine*　　ISBN: *1-59462-128-4*　**$29.95**
The chief object of the following pages is to indicate some of the earliest ideas of mankind, as they are reflected in Ancient Law, and to point out the relation of those ideas to modern thought.　　Religion/History Pages 452

Far-Away Stories by *William J. Locke*　　ISBN: *1-59462-129-2*　**$19.45**
"Good wine needs no bush, but a collection of mixed vintages does. And this book is just such a collection. Some of the stories I do not want to remain buried for ever in the museum files of dead magazine-numbers an author's not unpardonable vanity..."　　Fiction Pages 272

Life of David Crockett by *David Crockett*　　ISBN: *1-59462-250-7*　**$27.45**
"Colonel David Crockett was one of the most remarkable men of the times in which he lived. Born in humble life, but gifted with a strong will, an indomitable courage, and unremitting perseverance...　　Biographies/New Age Pages 424

Lip-Reading by *Edward Nitchie*　　ISBN: *1-59462-206-X*　**$25.95**
Edward B. Nitchie, founder of the New York School for the Hard of Hearing, now the Nitchie School of Lip-Reading, Inc, wrote "LIP-READING Principles and Practice". The development and perfecting of this meritorious work on lip-reading was an undertaking...　　How-to Pages 400

A Handbook of Suggestive Therapeutics, Applied Hypnotism, Psychic Science　　ISBN: *1-59462-214-0*　**$24.95**
by *Henry Munro*　　Health/New Age/Health/Self-help Pages 376

A Doll's House: and Two Other Plays by *Henrik Ibsen*　　ISBN: *1-59462-112-8*　**$19.95**
Henrik Ibsen created this classic when in revolutionary 1848 Rome. Introducing some striking concepts in playwriting for the realist genre, this play has been studied the world over.　　Fiction/Classics/Plays 308

The Light of Asia by *sir Edwin Arnold*　　ISBN: *1-59462-204-3*　**$13.95**
In this poetic masterpiece, Edwin Arnold describes the life and teachings of Buddha. The man who was to become known as Buddha to the world was born as Prince Gautama of India but he rejected the worldly riches and abandoned the reigns of power when...　　Religion/History/Biographies Pages 170

The Complete Works of Guy de Maupassant by *Guy de Maupassant*　　ISBN: *1-59462-157-8*　**$16.95**
"For days and days, nights and nights, I had dreamed of that first kiss which was to consecrate our engagement, and I knew not on what spot I should put my lips..."　　Fiction/Classics Pages 240

The Art of Cross-Examination by *Francis L. Wellman*　　ISBN: *1-59462-309-0*　**$26.95**
Written by a renowned trial lawyer, Wellman imparts his experience and uses case studies to explain how to use psychology to extract desired information through questioning.　　How-to/Science/Reference Pages 408

Answered or Unanswered? by *Louisa Vaughan*　　ISBN: *1-59462-248-5*　**$10.95**
Miracles of Faith in China　　Religion Pages 112

The Edinburgh Lectures on Mental Science (1909) by *Thomas*　　ISBN: *1-59462-008-3*　**$11.95**
This book contains the substance of a course of lectures recently given by the writer in the Queen Street Hall, Edinburgh. Its purpose is to indicate the Natural Principles governing the relation between Mental Action and Material Conditions...　　New Age/Psychology Pages 148

Ayesha by *H. Rider Haggard*　　ISBN: *1-59462-301-5*　**$24.95**
Verily and indeed it is the unexpected that happens! Probably if there was one person upon the earth from whom the Editor of this, and of a certain previous history, did not expect to hear again...　　Classics Pages 380

Ayala's Angel by *Anthony Trollope*　　ISBN: *1-59462-352-X*　**$29.95**
The two girls were both pretty, but Lucy who was twenty-one who supposed to be simple and comparatively unattractive, whereas Ayala was credited, as her Bombwhat romantic name might show, with poetic charm and a taste for romance. Ayala when her father died was nineteen...　　Fiction Pages 484

The American Commonwealth by *James Bryce*　　ISBN: *1-59462-286-8*　**$34.45**
An interpretation of American democratic political theory. It examines political mechanics and society from the perspective of Scotsman James Bryce　　Politics Pages 572

Stories of the Pilgrims by *Margaret P. Pumphrey*　　ISBN: *1-59462-116-0*　**$17.95**
This book explores pilgrims religious oppression in England as well as their escape to Holland and eventual crossing to America on the Mayflower, and their early days in New England...　　History Pages 268

QTY

The Fasting Cure by *Sinclair Upton*   ISBN: *1-59462-222-1*   **$13.95**
In the Cosmopolitan Magazine for May, 1910, and in the Contemporary Review (London) for April, 1910, I published an article dealing with my experiences in fasting. I have written a great many magazine articles, but never one which attracted so much attention... New Age/Self Help/Health Pages 164

Hebrew Astrology by *Sepharial*   ISBN: *1-59462-308-2*   **$13.45**
In these days of advanced thinking it is a matter of common observation that we have left many of the old landmarks behind and that we are now pressing forward to greater heights and to a wider horizon than that which represented the mind-content of our progenitors... Astrology Pages 144

Thought Vibration or The Law of Attraction in the Thought World   ISBN: *1-59462-127-6*   **$12.95**
by *William Walker Atkinson*   Psychology/Religion Pages 144

Optimism by *Helen Keller*   ISBN: *1-59462-108-X*   **$15.95**
Helen Keller was blind, deaf, and mute since 19 months old, yet famously learned how to overcome these handicaps, communicate with the world, and spread her lectures promoting optimism. An inspiring read for everyone... Biographies/Inspirational Pages 84

Sara Crewe by *Frances Burnett*   ISBN: *1-59462-360-0*   **$9.45**
In the first place, Miss Minchin lived in London. Her home was a large, dull, tall one, in a large, dull square, where all the houses were alike, and all the sparrows were alike, and where all the door-knockers made the same heavy sound... Childrens/Classic Pages 88

The Autobiography of Benjamin Franklin by *Benjamin Franklin*   ISBN: *1-59462-135-7*   **$24.95**
The Autobiography of Benjamin Franklin has probably been more extensively read than any other American historical work, and no other book of its kind has had such ups and downs of fortune. Franklin lived for many years in England, where he was agent... Biographies/History Pages 332

Name	
Email	
Telephone	
Address	
City, State ZIP	

☐ **Credit Card**   ☐ **Check / Money Order**

Credit Card Number	
Expiration Date	
Signature	

Please Mail to: Book Jungle
                  PO Box 2226
                  Champaign, IL 61825
or Fax to: 630-214-0564

www.ingramcontent.com/pod-product-compliance
Lightning Source LLC
Chambersburg PA
CBHW050353100426

42739CB00015BB/3380